From Sulphur Springs
to
Cowtown

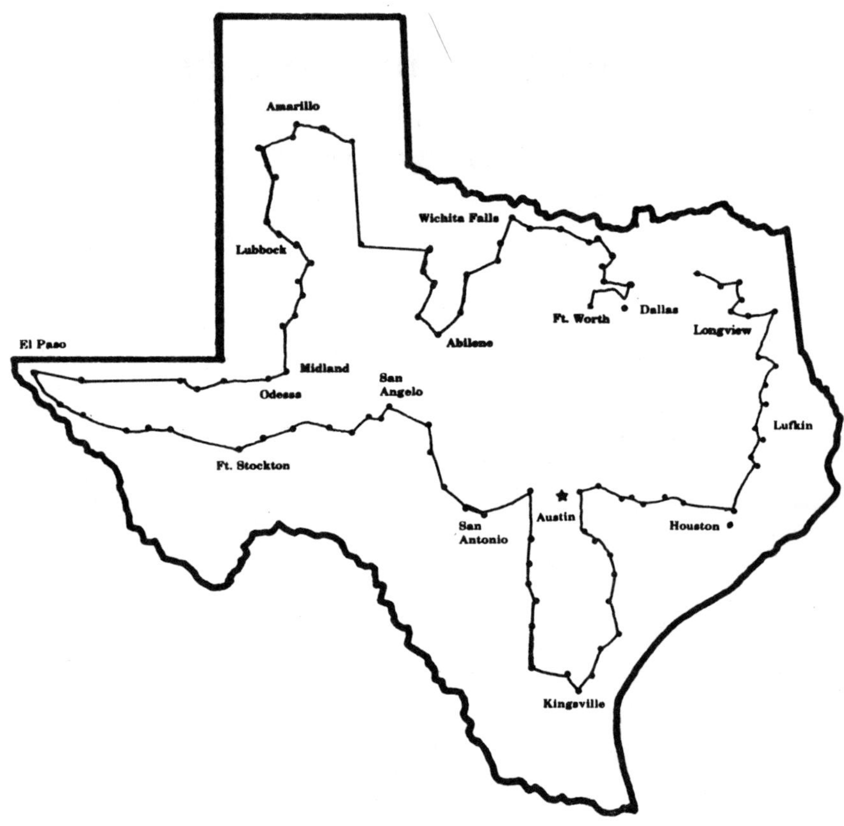

Amarillo
Wichita Falls
Lubbock
Ft. Worth
Dallas
Longview
Abilene
El Paso
Midland
San
Angelo
Lufkin
Odessa
Ft. Stockton
San
Antonio
Austin
Houston
Kingsville

From Sulphur Springs to Cowtown

*The Story
of the Sesquicentennial
1986 Texas Wagon Train*

Donna Neal Stepp

VANTAGE PRESS
New York / Los Angeles / Chicago

Copyright © 1987 by Donna Neal Stepp

Published by Vantage Press, Inc.
516 West 34th Street, New York, New York 10001

Manufactured in the United States of America
ISBN: 0-533-07504-1

Library of Congress Catalog Card No.: 87-90116

To my son, Danial, who made the entire journey in
my heart and on my mind.

With Appreciation

Suzanne Whitfield, of Stephenville, Texas, took all of the photographs within this book. After the event was completed she and her husband James moved to Edwards Airforce Base in California. Suzanne notified me in August of 1986 that I could have my pick of any of the more than 1000 slides she had taken on the Texas Wagon Train journey to put in my book. It is this type of kindness that prevailed amongst the wagoneers and brought us all together in the first place. Mrs. Whitfield hand delivered her work to me from California stating she wanted nothing in return. At the same time I return to her my heartfelt gratitude and admiration for an unselfish act of kindness that I can never truly repay.

From Sulphur Springs to Cowtown

Chapter One

Bobby Stepp and I were married April 10, 1984, and in August of that year he heard about the Texas Wagon Train on WBAP radio in Fort Worth. The journey was to go more than three thousand miles around the state of Texas and be on the road more than six months. In the beginning, I thought it would be great for me to ride into Fort Worth with the train from Wichita Falls, Texas; then I quickly changed my mind to Amarillo. The next day, I set my goal on riding the whole journey, and nothing could change my mind. For anyone to prepare to be away from home for six months at a time is not easy. Now I found myself telling my new husband that I was going away for a while, not the best domestic idea a wife can come up with after four months of wedded bliss. Bobby had no thoughts of coming along; he would visit me periodically, but riding on a horse or in a wagon for six months did not appeal to him whatsoever. I knew I was on my own. The first challenge was to get ready. I, along with other wagoneers, worked very hard long hours to be able to all meet in Sulphur Springs, Texas and roll out with the wagons on January 2, 1986.

I was a secretary at the Forth Worth Auto Auction plus I dealt cards and dice at Billy Bob's Texas in the stockyards, where ultimately the wagon train would come into at the end of the journey. Both of these jobs plus taking care of my new husband and the house on top of exercising my mare that was to go with me kept me very busy. The business college that I graduated from, also at the same time, was helping me improve my skills to find employment when I returned to civilization.

Joining the Texas Wagon Train Association was everyone's first step. Of the six thousand participants that were to ultimately sign up for the train, I was number eighteen. I just told everyone that I was a bit more anxious than most. There should have been a place on the application to fill in about one's state of mind to join this outfit. Now I know it was understood beforehand that we all had to be a bit off balance to even consider this adventure, let alone really do it. Lewis and Clark, Davey Crockett, and even Napoleon, were a group of strange people; trust me.

Texas was celebrating its 150th birthday. Everyone that wanted to was going to help her do it in the biggest way possible. Texas is known for BIG. This was to be no exception. To be able to participate was truly an honor; we knew people would want to join us and go along. We must have seen a million tears from those very same people. They couldn't go, so we were going to do it for them, with all of the pride, dedication, honor, and integrity we could get together and take down the highways and roadways of Texas. We would walk in the shadows of the men and women that went a century before us and laid the foundation for a state that will live long after any of us are gone because of the sacrifices these people, these original pioneers, made for us.

The wagons came from all over the United States: Virginia, Tennessee, Arkansas, Georgia, Oklahoma, New Mexico, and many, many more. They were volunteers that were here to help Texas once again, this time in the name of peace and laughter and glory, to reach out and touch our forefathers in the only way modern day man can do in the eighties—from a covered wagon train. The wagons represented the most authentic to that most modern: Green ones, red ones, and wagons with no color at all as the original wagons had been.Some were conastogas from out of the past. There were iron rims and wooden rims with rubber strips on them to travel better. Some of the wagons had modern day car tires on them. What with some of the participants being in their late seventies and eighties, it was to their comfort and added to their ability to travel with us to have these type of wagons. Altogether, one hundred seven wagons and two hundred ninety-one horseback riders were getting ready to leave Sulphur Springs on a journey of a lifetime that none of us would ever forget.

I chose to ride a horse throughout the journey, as I had made a commitment to write a book about the trip and did not want the responsibility of a wagon and a team of animals to take care of. I wanted to keep my freedom. I had to walk amongst the people to get to know them and work with them to get the material I wanted. My mare, Lady, was in her seventeenth year when we started this trek and I had owned her for ten years, so I felt I knew we could work together this way, too. I had ridden horses for thirty years when I started and thought I knew a lot; boy, did I learn real quick how much I didn't know!

In the 1880s, my great-grandfather, Otus Festus Neal, went to Oregon in a covered wagon. In my younger years, I would sit and daydream about what kind of adventures that journey must have presented to him and his family. I was born and raised in that state; my father was a lumberjack. Now there is a tough breed of man. In honor of him and my ancestors that took to the trails of pioneering, I left Forth Worth, Texas on December 31, 1985 to join eight hundred others, and walk more than three thousand miles around the great Lone Star State to celebrate freedom.

It was New Year's Eve and a "get acquainted" dance was being given to gather all of the participants together. I met Jan France for the first time at the dance. I recognized her voice, as we had spoken on the phone before, but had not met. She was much younger than I had thought, but just as pretty. Jan is the founder of the Texas Wagon Train.

With the balloons, and liquor flowing, at the stroke of midnight, I wished my new friends a very happy new year and went back to camp. A stranger walked by as I stepped outside. He tipped his hat and said, "Happy new year, ma'am. Do you know you're walking into history"?

"Yes, sir," I replied.

It was January 1, 1986. The wagons would roll tomorrow. The Sesquicentennial had begun. Our journey into history had started. Early on the first day of the new year I found myself walking out through the camp to see all I could. I wanted to meet everyone; not knowing a soul was bothering me. I was to travel very closely with these people for six months and didn't know a name. I had met a handful the night before and I would have to ask most of them their names again. In fact, I spent most of the first three months asking each one about nine times what their names were. No sense being embarrassed about it; just do it. Here we were, pioneers of the eighties, all setting off to do the same thing. It was fun walking amongst the camp to see every one getting ready. We knew we were the lucky ones, the chosen ones.

The pathways between the campsites quickly filled up with onlookers to reach out and touch the wagoneers. It did not take long to realize this trip was going to be in the limelight most of the way. Now there was an adjustment to come to terms with. Everywhere harnesses were being checked and rechecked; teams were being hooked up and worked. One thing about livestock, they cannot just stand around and be tied up on days that we do not travel, even if it is just for a little while. They must be exercised and worked with. This prevents them from becoming sore. We would all learn more about this further on down the trail.

The anvils of the blacksmiths were singing their songs of iron on iron. Everywhere you could see someone working on a part of their gear to get the wagons or their horses ready.

Not everyone was to be in a wagon. Many others had also chosen to ride a horse as I had. Paints, sorrels, palominos, bays, buckskins; you name it and it was there. No stallions or dogs were to be on the journey in an attempt to eliminate mass confusion, however there were many times that mass confusion was the normal daily routine.

As I walked about camp, I saw horseshoes being played and songs being sung by amateur musicians. The sounds were very comforting. Tales were being reminisced of other wagon trains in years gone by and of course this one that would roll very soon.

My mare would join me tonight and be a part of the rest of the livestock that would pass along the communications out through the campgrounds in the early morning hours. That would be our alarm clock for the next six months. It seemed to me that the entire state was waiting for us and I knew we were as ready right then as we could possibly be.

Chapter Two

Lady had come in during the night; I went to sleep worrying if she would make it or not. I crawled out of my tent to see her standing across the road from me. My husband was sleeping in the truck.

The wagons would roll in two hours, and I was still trying to believe I was going to do this. Many thought I had lost all sense of reality by even attempting such an event as this. My grandfather made it; why couldn't I?

Due to changing my gear around and a last minute nature call, the entire wagon train had left camp and I had to run to catch up. Garry France had thrown back his head for the first time and yelled: "Wagons Ho!" I could not stop the tears and the warm feelings that raced all the way through me. What a sound! One hundred seven wagons and two hundred ninety-one saddle horses rode out of Sulphur Springs, Texas on January 2, 1986. Jan France was driving the lead wagon, with Gov. Mark White right beside her. We were on our way.

The horseback riders had to follow the last wagon in line; in this case, it was a buggy. In doing so, we missed most of the fanfare that went on at the lead of the wagon train. This would be the rule of thumb throughout the entire journey. We did not grow accustomed to it; it was just somethig that had to be. However, the people along the roadway that were always there to see the wagon train, and always there to wave and smile and in many cases touch us, were there in back as well as the front. Such was the housewife just outside of Sulphur Springs with her two small ones wrapped up in some type of tent but with their two little heads showing, so as not to miss this awesome moment; or the ranch hands near Como that rode up to the fence to watch in silence. Then there was an elderly lady that seemed to lean heavily on the glassed front door with visions of years gone by and tales that must have been told to her when she was young. I waved to her and a youthful smile that I felt had not been there for many many years came across that face.

We traveled on that day. People lined the streets just

to have a glimpse of the modern day wonder as it passed by. I believe the same thought must have crossed the observers' minds as it did ours. Even though we were doing this, was it really real? A locomotive came into view near Como. The engineer waved at the train going the opposite way. A train from the past met a train of present. The signs along the way wished us well, and safety, and happy trails. We would shed many tears over this journey through the next six months; it appeared to me that there was no getting around that. For the shadows we were walking in, how could we not? Not many of the wagoneers slept outside as I was doing. There were many motor homes with all the conveniences of home. Not everyone can sleep in the elements of the great out-of-doors.

You can ride for miles every day and prepare yourself for what you believe to be the right kind of atmosphere, but until the actual event starts, no kind of mockup can get you there like the real thing. We did not ride far the first day, only fifteen miles, but we were a very weary group. For those who didn't have anyone to move their support vehicles to the new camp, they caught the shuttle bus to go back to the old camp to get the motorhomes, trailers, and campers to move them forward to the new camp. The livestock always came first bar none. Unsaddle, unharness, whatever the case may be, the horses and mules were the first to be taken care of. Now there were many on this journey that knew God had a hand above us all the time.

I have to agree with any and all that voiced this opinion: Texas weather leaves much to be desired. But as the old saying goes: "If you don't like the weather just wait twenty minutes and it will change." Well, as chance would have it, most of us from here in Texas locations that came to join the wagon train remember the weather from last winter. It was horrible and most cold. The weather in Sulphur Springs was around sixty-five and very comfortable for a day's ride. We just thought we had hit it lucky for the day, but we would soon see that the weather would hold in our favor almost every day of the entire journey.

Chapter Three

The second day found the pioneers of the eighties traveling into Winnsboro, down into the valley where the wagons were circled with trees close by. The crowd of welcomers were as warm as before, smiles to greet us and tears to show us that they cared. It was easy to let your thoughts go back in time and know a little of how the first settlers felt and thought as they came over a rise to see what was on the other side so they would be safe for another day. Riding in the back of the wagon train, we did not see the wagons together until we came over the hill. There before us was the complete circle. Later I found out that Jan France stood by her lead wagon watching the train come over the hill and shed her tears to see it's magnificence. I shed mine when I saw it suddenly before me as I rode over last.

Early the next morning around four-thirty, I walked down amongst the covered wagons before the sun came up to see the canvas covered ghosts standing there, waiting to receive their loads of passengers and to be made ready for the day. As I stood there in total wonderment at what I had gotten myself into, I knew that if only America could see what I was seeing now they would all be as proud of their roots and know that the lives lost on battlefields were not lost in vain. I believe a light was shining from last century at that moment in time, and you could just barely see it from over the hill.

Our third day of travel found us beginning to tire, but we knew this and just went to bed earlier. Some of the tough ones still partied and danced at the celebrations given us, but I was not one of them. I really wanted to, but I started this journey thirty-five pounds overweight and it was weighing about ten pounds more than that right now.

The weather had become colder during the night. This was our coldest night yet, twenty-two degrees. But I was still very comfortable with my outdoor accommodations. The water pipes froze, and we had to find someone with a stove to heat existing water to get the faucets to work so we could water the livestock. Yes, winter had set in and we were in for some rough traveling, but we still did not have any snow or freezing rain. The hill we were on did not give us a break from the cold wind that blew through you if you did not wear clothing.

We were looking at a twenty-six mile day today. Everyone was exhausted. The wagon master's son, Cody France, was thrown from his horse today when the animal reared straight up and came down right on top of him. I was riding beside him and was sure that Cody would be crushed to death as the horse could not get his balance and get off of Cody. After close examination, the boy was shaken up, but no serious injury befell him.

An hour and half after we pitched camp, I had watered Lady and fed her, then tied her to a friend's trailer. My tent was pitched about five feet from her. I stepped inside, then noticed Lady stomping on my tent. I hurried outside to observe her shivering all over and throwing herself on the ground. She was in serious trouble and I had to do something as fast as I could. I untied her and tried to lead her. She would take a step or two and again fall to the ground. I was really worried for her because where I was camped, I could not leave her to go for help. She would rear, then thrash on the ground again. I saw an opening between the fence and a big diesel truck. Lady hasn't gone through small places in the ten years I've owned her. I knew Dr. Ken, the vet, was camped across the road from me and the quickest way to his place was through that narrow opening. Lady came through it right behind me and I rushed her to the vet's as fast as I could, pulling and coaxing.

Pounding on the door brought about Dr. Ken's assistant, Bruce, who did not know the whereabouts of the vet. Lady, still thrashing, needed immediate attention. Just then, Dr. Ken drove around the corner; he took one look at Lady and ran to the vet box in the back of his truck and grabbed a syringe full of whatever was necessary to treat the mare. He also aced (tranquilized) her, then put her in a shoot to hold her up and still. Twelve quarts of liquid later and a gallon of oil in the stomach brought her out of the colic problem perfectly. The twelve quarts had to be dripped in through a main vein in her neck. She had colicked, dehydrated, and went into shock all at the same time.

The next morning, Lady and I were ready to go. Garry France asked me if I would like to ride scout for the second wagon, Hazel Bowen's wagon. I accepted and rode up the line to take my assigned place for the day. Hazel is seventy-eight, and drove the same wagon in the Bicentennial wagon train pilgrimmage from Houston, Texas to Valley Forge, Pennsylvania in 1976.

Chapter Four

Scout riders were responsible for watering the stock and helping the drivers of the wagons they are scouting for in any capacity necessary. Hazel Bowen has had a pair of lines in her hands for seventy-three of the seventy-eight years she's been around. Therefore I felt no matter what she said to me, I best pay close attention. On this particular journey, that was good advice I gave myself.

Later, after we had our lunch stop, the wagon master had to fall back and take care of a problem. His son Rowdy was left to lead the train. However, he too had to fall back. That left me, as the command goes right down the line. Lady and I went to the lead of the train, and I can say I felt privileged. It was cold on this afternoon, so the people along the roadway were not plentiful, but I knew my ancestors could see me and I was proud.

Cold weather didn't seem to slow the wagon train down or even make the participants complain. The original settlers of this state had walked the same way, maybe without precut roadways and definitely without the fanfare, but with the same sense of accomplishment.

The wagon train traveled along for five days before the first lay over rest stop was scheduled. What a relief it was to just get up on that second day. Though it was five in the morning, it was nice to know that we could go back and catch an hour's rest or more if we wanted to. I can't speak for the entire camp, but we were so crammed into camp in Longview that it was easy to see I was not the only wagoneer taking advantage of the rest day. For the two-night, one-whole-day layover, many school children came to walk out through the wagons on the circle, then continue on to ask questions of the participants. It was always a treat for both the visitors and the pioneers to have questions asked and to show folks big and little just what it took to get the wagon train down the road. Yes, our modern day equipment such as the blue rooms (outhouses), water tanks, and staff to answer our questions and keep us in contact with the directors was not what the pioneers of a century ago had, but it was our way.

Also, as far as taking the entire train down the road, we were on our own. The teams were harnessed, horses saddled, and gear made ready for each day's trip without benefit of anyone, except the wagoneers, getting this outfit on its daily way.

Traveling into Longview, I rode in Miss Hazel's wagon. Lady didn't look right to me, so I gave her the day off and hopped a wagon. Right after lunch, the covered wagon that followed Miss Hazel's wagon had a slight encounter with us. I was sitting in the last bench seat on the wagon when I heard a loud noise from behind me. I turned just in time to see one of the hitch horses of Billy Bob's sponsored wagon ram right into the back of Miss Hazel's wagon. That particular four-up hitch were all paint draft horses. From my viewpoint, the two lead horses became separated and went two directions, while the wheel team just wanted to run as fast as they could anywhere. Miss Hazel's team took off like the typical bat from a hot place. The scout riders for the Billy Bob wagon jumped into action to help the driver, Leo Miller. The wagon I was in, being pulled by a big team of Belgians, also became a trouble spot. The Belgians ran in fright, having blinders on. This team did not know that the incident behind was under control. The wagon master spurred his mount on to catch us; we had passed the lead wagon and were on our way down the highway. The onlookers along the roadway were treated to some exciting action shots as the two teams became momentarily out of control and needed very sure experienced hands to calm them. I did the only thing I could think of—I took pictures. . . .

We had a two-night stay in this community and a welcome one at that. Harnesses needed to be repaired, stock had to be shod, and just general rest was needed, not to mention the laundry was do.

Since leaving Sulphur Springs, the wagon train had been received by the public with open arms, well wishes, and appreciation that cannot be matched anywhere in the world at this point. Garry France rode back with the outriders behind the last wagon one day. He shared stories of his birthplace, Sulphur Springs, and how he and his wife, Jan, felt about this train. We enjoyed his time with us.

As we rolled down some backwoods country roads toward Marshall, Texas, I let my thoughts wander back again as I would so often on this journey, to the original settlers riding through cold seasons in search of what they were looking for for their families. Most of the trees were without leaves, the underbrush was sparse, and the covered wagons all made a squeeking rattle as we traveled along. It was my forty-forth birthday and I had not felt this good in years. At the same time I was more tired than I had been in my entire life.

In camp, the Smith family hosted us with loving care. My tent was pitched down by the lake under the big trees. Again we had a two-night camp one-free-day layover.

Now I had not been around mules until I came on this trip, but it was easy to see that these animals are to be recognized. Someone left two mules still in harness tied to a wagon when we arrived in camp at Rosebourough Springs. I was walking by and saw one of the mules catch his headgear, in this case a bridle, on part of the wagon. This mule was standing at an odd angle; its hind quarters where higher than its front quarters, therefore the pulling angle was at its best. That mule gave a tug and it looked like the whole outfit was going to be overturned. A stranger came from out of the crowd and began talking to the mule. The animal calmed down enough to where the man reached and unhooked the bridle from where it was caught and allowed the mule his freedom. What was interesting to me was that the mule knew this stranger was going to help, and got down on his knees to relieve the pressure so he was able to be set free. The stranger walked away and I had learned another lesson about animals, especially mules.

I was looking for Bobby to show up sometime today, but my birthday was spent alone. The VFW from Paris, Texas, said they would bring me a cake also, but someone else must have eaten it. Because I lived outside, it was uncomfortable for me to be indoors very long, as I began to roast with all the clothes I had on. I walked over to the dance, as I wanted to shuffle at least once around the room on my birthday. I was asked by Doug Medlin, our chief assistant wagon master, to waltz and accepted. What a sight we must have been, in my Early American big brown western hat with my homemade blanket coat on, flowing around the dance floor. Doug stands about a foot taller than I am and had his usual western wear on also. It was fun and I felt like I had really celebrated. Cold, I wandered back to camp, checked on my mare, and turned in. The chill in the air made me just want to curl up and sleep until it was over. Plus I felt every bit of my years; this pioneer was exhausted. Lady and I had both been kicked solidly that day, and I was afraid that an injury would show up as the day progressed. Luck was with us; we both escaped serious wounds. Someone was watching.

We seemed to be blessed with short days riding in the cold weather. Actually, while the sun was out, it was not at all cold, plus we were traveling south toward Houston and warmer temperatures. As soon as we rolled into camp that day near Clayton, Mr. Macy Nelson fell to the ground quite ill. It is easy to rush to the aid of someone that you want to help, but we held back to let the professional staff do their work. Mr. Nelson had had a recent bout with cancer, coupled with losing his wife. The journey was full of very hard work as well as responsibility. Mr. Nelson is up in years and more than likely had pushed himself to the limits of strain, as we all had. Our prayers were with him. A huge campfire was built to bring everyone together. The covered wagons circled and the pioneers sat around the blaze. It made us all warmer inside and out. Singing began and continued throughout the night. Jan brought out her songbooks, for we all seemed to forget the words on the same line.

Bobby had come to visit me and I was sure glad to see him.

Up until now, we had traveled on some pretty even roadways. Some of the route turned into hills but not enough to strain a muscle. Upon leaving Clayton toward Mount Enterprise, we met the challenge of a few hills straight on. Our route was most scenic, but the last mile proved to be demanding. The teams in harness met the test full force, and the wagons came up those hills real smooth. Once again we were reminded of the days long ago when everyone looked over his or her shoulder to make sure someone else didn't need their help in whatever capacity it would take to get to camp safely.

New shoes were required for my mare. I had borium added to the shoes, as it prevented the foot from slipping on the pavement. Actually, I do not like borium. It interferes with the natural growth of the hoof, I feel. But I decided it was necessary. We were camped in a large cow pasture and it looked like the generators would run all night long. The big motors with their continuous humming as loud as an airplaine engine would keep some awake while lulling others into a deep slumber.

The public was out in force as we arrived that night. They were armed with their ever present cameras. At the same time, it was amazing what a covered wagon train circled in a large cow pasture, coated with cow manure, will do to the public. We became accustomed to the everyday existence of the animal waste, but we were also aware of those that believed we were a little insensitive to the presence of such matter surrounding us at all times. They were absolutely correct. We did not at any time get bothered with having horse manure on our hands, clothes, boots, buckets, or anything else we handled twenty-four hours a day. It was quiet simply an accepted part of the wagon train.

Throughout the entire journey, there were two major questions asked whenever the train pulled into camp. Both always about showers and hot running water—a rare thing out on the trail. Just go on a little camping expedition around your town. This particular commodity is not just a wagon train inconvenience. I stood for thirty minutes in the cold wind waiting for the shuttle bus to come and pick myself and several others up for a nice hot shower, but I'm sure the traffic blocking the entrance to the campground had a lot to do with the bus not getting back to get us, so we went to our quarters without the benefit of a shower that night. It wouldn't be the last time. Just a few days out on the trail and we were making adjustments to pioneering ways very easily.

Texas, being a large state, afforded us the sight of many different kinds of surroundings all around us as the trip progressed into the six months. Going to the oldest town in the state, Nacogdoches, we spent the whole day on the pavement alongside the interstate. On one corner we saw many, many school students standing along the roadway holding little Texas flags. They must have spent a week in class to make them. What a precious sight they were. Not a single one of them waved his or her flag as we passed by. Later I was told they were all instructed to hold the flags still so as not to disturb the livestock as we passed by. Now these children were only in the first and second grades, as well as kindergarten. So it is most important that they get credit where credit is due. For such young people to stand so still for so long and not wave a flag that they made themselves is to be commended highly. Kids, I'm proud of you!

The wagon train usually traveled on the extreme right side of the highways and interstates. We rarely got up on the interstates because of the traffic congestion that the train always caused wherever we went, but there were times that in order to get to the campgrounds, there simply was no other way. Most of the saddle horses walked in the bar ditches, the grassey area alongside the highways, and the teams were almost always on the pavement.

Twelve miles out of Nacogdoches, I was asked to carry the Texas flag into this fine old city. Susan Venus, our schoolteacher and resident from this town, carried the city flag. Susan, I know, was most proud of the wagon train, Nacogdoches, and to be carrying that flag.

Five miles out of town, we stopped to pick up the mayor of Nacogdoches and Senator Parks. All of the area dignitaries along the entire route usually rode into their towns from just outside of their city limits in the lead wagon, driven by Jan France, our executive director. It is unfortunate, at the same time, that I must say something about the rest of the wagon train that never saw the programs and special ceremonies along the trail because they were traveling in the back of the train. If it were ever possible to double the lines or triple the wagons up to allow these wagoneers to see the presentations at the lead of the train, it was done. I chose to ride a horse on the journey as I mentioned before because of the freedom it allowed. But it wasn't really until we were into the trip that I knew how good of a decision that was. I did not at any time feel that the people in the rear of the train were any less important than the travelers in front. However, it always bothered me that so much was missed out on by the back wagoneers.

Just about every day someone was thrown, or fell off, or fell with a horse. Our traveling medical staff was always at hand to see to the victim at once, but the accidents did occur on a daily basis. Hank Johnson fell that day and we were very anxious for a few moments, as the accident occurred at the rear of the train. As I mentioned before, the front can't always know what is going on at the back. We all noticed Hank's horse runing up the highway like a bat out of hell and an empty saddle flapping on its back. One of the staff riders caught the animal and returned it to Hank and we learned that he was not injured seriously. But of course a rider's dignity always damages.

The people of Nacogdoches offered us a tour of their city. It is the home of the Stephen F. Austin University and the first town of Texas and has many interesting sites. Our school students always made historical journeys and tours to aid in their education and add to their history, but the adults were not afforded that privilege often, so we took advantage of this service whenever possible. Being a history buff, I was first to inquire about departure time. Our bus was loaded as many were very interested in this, the earliest community in Texas. Dressed in our wagon train clothing, we presented quite a picture ourselves. The tour was fabulous, and we had a good time. The evening meal was provided for us, and such good hot food. The cold weather could be tolerated with a hot meal.

Fiddle players, guitar pickers, and someone with a mouth harp came to entertain us that night around our campfire. We were parked under a large tree, and I was given the distinct honor of pitching my tent with the staff people because I was just a "woman" traveling alone. Oh well, it's better to join them than to fuss over it. The musicians brought singers and others to accompany them. The music flowed out over the campground, a beautiful nite of old country music and songs that dated back to a century ago.

Olive Talley of the *Houston Post* offered to let me use her shower in the room she had for the night. I made the decision while running for my bag of shower gear.

Chapter Five

Most of the horses and mules had started to reprofile. Those that were too fat had lost the unnecessary flab and those that needed to tone up were starting to look real good. Some had to be laid off because the schedule that we had to keep was too hard for them to keep up with. Lady was still going good, but every so often I gave her a day off and found another horse to ride, or else I rode in a wagon. Most of the wagoneers brought a remount, or an alternate team to replace the others as they traveled along. I brought just Lady. Margaret Renz brought one mount, as did Willie Hazelwood and a couple more. At the end of the trail, two riders had ridden the entire way, but no horse had made the whole journey without being given more rest than what we had already scheduled.

The original settlers where brought to mind so many many times as the days progressed. We thought of what day of the week it was. The date and time was broken down to feeding time, eating time, traveling time, and bedtime. When you are traveling and as busy as we all were every single day of the week, you simply did not know what time, date, or what anything else it was. Radios were not common, nor were T.V.'s. Newspapers were not always available. Most of us did not have the time to sit and catch up. One afternoon, a rider called to me and asked what day it was. I thought it was Monday or Tuesday but I said to hold on I would check with another. His reply was Thursday or Friday. Now everyone within earshot was confused, so we went and checked with a traveler that we knew would know. To our surprise, it was Wednesday.

Shoeing horses every single day was a necessary thing on the wagon train. Boyd Ivey was the official blacksmith. He had made a big wagon with rubber tires to go on the trip, carrying all of his supplies with him. Boyd, one of the friendliest people anyone would want to meet anywhere in the world, would wait up very late at night, sometimes just to shoe someone's horse that just had to ride the next day. They would often not get their mounts to Boyd's place until almost midnight, but he still met them with a smile and a kind word and shod their horse or mule for them with the same kind of enthusiasm he did when he had a lot of rest. This man was truly an asset to the entire wagon train, and a fine representative from De Kalb, Texas. I would guess Boyd's age to be around forty-eight. He told me this was the first time in his entire life that he had been away from his own mailbox.

The usual accident for a rider occurred just outside of camp as a mule dumped its rider after jumping over a mud puddle. A young man from Louisiana, Sal, was unsaddling his and his partner's horse right after we came into camp when one of the horses threw his head ever so slightly but caught Sal right across the forehead. I heard

gelding, and could ride all day and never complain as many did. He talked all the time and quite frankly, he rode many right into the ground. At three and a half years old, he's going to really make a hand someday.

People lined the highway almost the entire way. Such faces we saw. In passing a retirement hospital, many of the residents were outside to view the wagons. The spirit that came from that group showed us they all have a long way to go yet. I started looking for Bobby to show up that day. My woman's intuition told me to expect him.

Just outside of Livingston, Texas we picked up a distinguished guest to ride in the lead wagon, Fulton Batieste. He had been the chief of the Alabama Coushattas tribe of Indians there in the area for fifty-five years. I shook his hand in greeting and he made a very proud statement. His words were, "It is good that I ride on the wagon train." He was dressed in his full tribal costume and made a striking figure in the wagon.

Later on, during the evening entertainment, the chief's tribe came to provide us with ceremonial dances from way back in the years of time. I walked out into the circle of wagons. The war drums began to beat, the canvas covers on the wagons were silhoueted in the moonlight, tall piney wood trees stood by silently as the night air carried out across that circle the beats of a tribe that had perhaps at one time been against the white man, now played only for entertainment. Yes, our pioneers where safe, our wagons in no danger, but very easily I could see into last century again and appreciate the fact that I and my friends of this wagon train would sleep in peace. I turned to go back to my camp. Bobby was walking across the open area toward me; I could just make out his familiar walk in the darkness.

Chapter Seven

The state and city and county officers that helped us through their areas are to be thanked many times over as we made our way around the state. They were always there and always helpful. Many times they were stationed near a spot that ended up being a runaway sight. It is not an everyday occasion for a peace officer nowadays to have a lot of experience in runaway teams, as our horses and mules had. It was always with humor to me that they were the first ones to take a picture or a video, then put on the serious look of authority and continue on with the traffic problems the wagon train created continuously. Two officers in east Texas were to stay alongside the train on a busy highway as we stopped for a water break. Four large one thousand gallon tanks accompanied us and were placed at the necessary spots to water the stock when it was time, usually every two hours. Meanwhile the officers were not going to be done out of any pictures.

A guest rider on the second wagon I was riding in, and myself, could not wait for the blue rooms (outhouses) to show up, so we opted to hike back to them. We were about fifty feet from the facility when one of the officers began to ask us questions about the journey. We were trying to be descreet and let him know that we were not the best subjects he could have in focus at the moment. Finally, when we realized there was not to be any reprieve, I said, "We are on our way to the blue room, and will chat with you in just a bit." Having a microphone on his moving camera, I thought this was good enough. Not so, he wanted to know just what we were talking about. So I accommodated, with, "We're on our way to the bathroom, we'll be with you in just a moment." He was very embarrassed. That's show biz!

All kidding aside, the police force was always helpful. For example, there was the time a particular group guided us through traffic tie ups and major intersections, rerouting, and getting us out of just plan jams. They had to leave us at the county line. Four deep blue official vehicles made a U-turn and with arms extended out the drivers' windows, we heard a warming message as they drove out of sight, "Good luck, ya'll. We wish you a safe journey." They were as proud of us as we had been of them. That's what this journey was all about: human kindness and appreciation.

Right after that, I was standing near Lady at a water break. All of a sudden, fire ants began to bite me all over. I was hopping up and down like a bunny. Somebody yelled to see if I was all right. Someone else was brushing me off all over and I let it be known that if I couldn't get out of this mess, everyone was fixin' to see a wagoneer strip plumb naked to save herself. Nothing but laughing and encouragement came on behalf of the ants, but I made it through the episode fully clothed, and my dignity intact.

Chapter Eight

Crossing the Livingston Reservoir was an interesting day. We took the saddle horses across first, leading them at all times. Then the wagons came behind with someone leading each team member. The roadway across the dam was narrow, twelve feet. No head of livestock had ever been across the dam in the history of the facility. We were about to change that record real quick. The big generators were shut off so as not to send any of the horses or mules into a fit of fright. The news media was asked to stay back out of the way as the wagons and animals crossed over the dam, for the helicopters would frighten also. Boats were alongside the wagons in the water, but out far enough not to cause concern. A large opening alongside the crossing was covered with heavy metal screening, but Lady took one look at it and became very nervous. I was leading her, as we all were, and just reached up to pat that curious head bobbing like a frightened child. It calmed her and we went with the flow.

The dismounted riders led the stock about a mile. Then, turning, we were gifted with a magnificent sight. Wagon after wagon rolled onto and off of the dam. The public was with us on the top and bottom side of the dam. The crossing had gone smoothly. Only one team refused to step out on the passageway. We knew they couldn't hear us from so far away where we had led our horses to wait, but we all urged and coaxed that team. Holding our breath, we waited what must have been two minutes but seemed to be ten. The gap in the wagon train had grown to about one hundred feet, and we thought there would be panic amongst the animals if that team didn't move. Those mules decided not to be left behind and began to step on out to join the others. We cheered loudly and kept urging them on. We had been given orders not to mount up until the last wagon rolled off of the passageway over the dam area. The last generator was passed; the wagons were safe and we remounted. The news media came in force, but not too close as we were still on a very narrow roadway with drop-offs on each side. We came through the private gates of that road and I was the first woman to ride a horse across Livingston Reservoir. Landle Cathcart was right beside me and Margaret and Vern Renz directly behind us. The crowds had gathered to greet us. Everyone was safe and our walk into history was making us most proud.

Our campsite was beautiful: waterfront camps, showers, and lots of room. Pam Blancset may not have been as thrilled as the rest of us, however, when the sun went down. Pam always prided herself on cleanliness and staying attractive for that special guy she hoped to meet somewhere along the trail. She had enjoyed a good shower and late meal, then walked to a fallen tree to look out across the campgrounds. With the moon reflecting on the water, it was a perfect setting to just think over the events of the day. Suddenly she heard footsteps close by and knew she had walked up the hill alone. Turning ever so slowly, she looked right at a skunk. Jumping into the air and yelling at full volume, she raced into camp out of breath and shaking all over. I believe she changed her cologne. Obviously the one she had on wasn't doing the job right!

Chapter Nine

We always seemed to travel on the pavement, never escaping its ever present hardness and dangers. This was understood beforehand, but when you are actually into the situation, you can see the negtive parts of it. In our case, it was so hard on the livestock's legs and feet.

We traveled about ten miles out of Camilia camp, then turned into a large parking lot South of Cold Springs. The facility was new and we didn't realize it was a water break—one that would possibly be the very best we would have anywhere on the journey. Twenty-four ladies of the community, volunteers, had brought to us every kind of homemade cookie ever invented plus hot coffee, fresh juice, prime fruits, and lemonade. The building was actually a country western dance hall. But it had been transformed into a warm greeting place for the wagoneers. Live entertainment came from a very young girl singing old western songs to our sheer pleasure. Someone had taken the time to videotape our crossing of the Livingston Reservoir; this too was put on a monitor and we watched ourselves take the history making steps across the dam. All of our hostesses were dressed in costumes of the 1800s era. I hope those ladies know how much we all loved them for coming to us from their homes just to welcome us and be there when the wagons rolled in. They kept telling us what a favor we were doing for them. It was almost a running argument throughout the whole journey as to who was the most glad who was there to meet who.

The pioneers of the eighties left those wonderful ladies and others that had dropped by to visit. We left out through a backwoods red dirt road into the San Jacinto National Forest. As we pulled away from that parking lot, the same ladies stepped out of the back door, lined up, and sang songs to us as we passed before them into the forest.

The sight of the wagons and us rolling down a narrow dirt road without cars or trucks or anything will be in our memories forever. Cotton Williams, secure in leaving the lines to the mules hanging from the front bow, crawled to the back of the wagon and yodled out through the timber to the delight of everyone within earshot. The rolling wheels squeeking along, the horse's and mule's hooves were silenced by the deep red dirt on the roadway. We passed such beauty: open little valleys, narrow old wooden bridges, ancient-looking homes that I later learned date back to Civil War times when the slaves were given this land by their owners when they were freed after the war was over.

A retired schoolteacher, Freddie Hughes, came into our camp after we circled the wagons. She walked amongst us with the sparkle of a child in her eye. At age seventy-five, she kept saying to us that she was having the time of her life just being there with the wagoneers. She and Mr. Hughes lived just down the road from where we were staying the night, on land that was given to her grandfather in 1860. If one can stop and absorb this, Mrs. Hughes lived on land that was given to her family twenty-four years after Santa Anna was captured in the San Jacinto Forest at the bend in the river just down the road from her home. The pioneers of the eighties were touching back to those original settlers again.

Chapter Ten

One more day's march brought us to the Houston area. It wasn't easy for us to believe we were doing this. It seemed outside opinions that kept filtering into our ears shared the same thought. Every day was easier and easier. People found it unbelievable for us to keep going on into the cold outdoor elements, living literally like gypsys. Our wagon train traveled over three thousand miles in six months and never missed any town or meeting spot that we were scheduled to meet. If anyone thinks about a force over five hundred strong traveling in the manner of which we were, that was a true accomplishment.

Upon arriving into camp, we learned there were two rooms reserved for us at the Holiday Inn to provide us with our showers. The people of Conroe had placed themselves solidly in our hearts. Hot running water did it every time. Pickup trucks loaded to the hilt with tired, weary travelers cut a pathway to the hot showers. We were to stay in Conroe for two days, so we put on our best smiles and clean shirts and looked forward to the nights' activities. Later, a band provided some of the best music and entertainment we would have along the trail. Old Hank Williams and Bob Wills tunes kept the dance floor full way into the late night hours. The wagon master and his wife, our seventy-eight year young oldster, and everyone else was waltzing and two-stepping into the night.

One of the newspaper reporters along the way asked us what we did on a layover day. When I told her we repaired wagons, wheels, tack, and exercised the stock, she was stunned at the thought of not resting the animals on a day of rest. I explained to her it was to the horses' and mules' benefit to keep their muscles moving to avoid stiffness and strain. I, along with Laurie McGown, Doug Medlin, Nelda French, and Mike Orr saddled up the second morning and rode out into the forest that lay between our camp near the airport and the downtown area of Conroe. It was a magnificent morning and we really enjoyed that quiet time. Laurie was not an experienced rider and she ended up with a spoiled horse. However, being the trouper she was, what she lacked in horsemanship she damn sure made up for in common sense.

The previous night, Nelda French and I had gone to the liquor store to get a bottle of liquor. The way she and I drank one bottle would last the both of us the next two thousand miles. The selection took a while as we could not agree on the same thing. However, we took a lot of ribbing from the guys—the drinkers—and ended up with a bottle of tequila from Mexico—with a worm in it! We found out the hard way it was potent stuff. Early the next morning, I got the bright idea to separate the little worm from the liquid and send it to school with one of the students as I knew they were studying bugs and insects. Just because one is forty-four years old, that is no indication the tricks are all gone out of the soul. I went in search of a student, grabbed the first one I saw, Reka France, and told her what I was up to. Later I found out none of the three teachers could figure out where in the world that worm came from; they had to be told. Dirty tricks lived and breathed on the wagon train.

Chapter Eleven

Montgomery rang the church bells as we passed by. There was always something heartwrenching whenever this happened for us. A silence would fall over the train momentarily, and we would all thank God for another day; there wasn't any other way to see it. Tears would fall throughout the journey because of the welcomers, the bells, the honor we all felt toward what we were doing, and many personal reasons expressed openly or never mentioned. The very first town that rang the bells for the wagoneers was Cold Springs, just outside of the San Jacinto Forest. It's strange how some things are never forgotten.

The wagons were pulled onto a ranch on January twenty-fourth for our lunch stop. All of the wagons except Morrison Milling's from Denton, Texas, moved into the fenced in area. Livestock from the ranch was loose so the gates were shut behind the last wagon. Fred and David Shivers, their wives, Debbie and Teresa, plus their four small girls all lived in the Morrison wagons throughout the entire journey. The brothers and their wives shared the chores and driving responsibilities. A five-horse draft hitch pulled the load. One of the hitch horses on the wheel, right in front of the wagon, had become ill. The hitch was set up with three horses directly in front of the wagon. These were called wheelers, and two more horses in the front were called leaders. The right wheeler was removed and another horse put in its place to help pull on into camp. This was done whenever any animal was having a problem.

Our vet, Dr. Ken Carlson, was always at hand to take care of the stock that was pulled out and needed transport to camp. He met the train five times a day with his stock trailer with all the necessary supplies to aid a sick animal when needed.

The new horse, offered by Albert Nicely of Goshen, Virginia, was put in the hitch, whereupon the beast promptly stuck his leg on the wrong side of the trace line. In trying to correct this, all hell broke loose. Debbie Shivers was sitting in the spring seat with her three little girls beside her. Debbie is Fred's wife; she had all of the lines in her hands. Teresa, David's wife, was between the wagons preparing lunch from the chuck box. Her daughter, Abbra, was in the back wagon also in the spring seat. Morrison Milling had two wagons being pulled in tandem. Fred and Debbie in the front wagon and David and Teresa in the second wagon. David and Fred were both on the ground working with the team. The new horse in the hitch was unfamiliar with everyone working with him and spooked when his leg was touched to move it back. The entire five-horse hitch spooked and ran. I was standing along with everyone else, eating my lunch inside the fenced area. I turned quickly at the unusual noise just in time to see the five-up hitch racing in a total panic toward the barbed wire fence. Debbie still had the lines in her hands with her leg over to the side to keep her babies from falling out of the wagon when it hit. At that point, it looked like the team was going through the wire. Fred was running and being dragged at the same time to try to stop the runaways. Horses that were tied to the fence began to panic. They broke their lead lines any way they could. The runaways were at top speed with no sign of slowing. The wagoneers and the livestock all stood in utter shock for a frozen moment. I can remember saying, "Oh shit." Then I dropped everything in my hands and ran to try to help catch the loose horses and release others that were fighting their lines to get free. Just then, the frightened runaways made a sudden left turn. Fred was thrown away from the team at this point. The chuck boxes on the wagons had begun to spill their contents everywhere. The running horses did not slow a bit at the turn. They had turned down alongside the same fence we thought they were going to run through. All of the loose stock inside the fence were going crazy from the confusion. The runaways turned again, this time to the right. The side boxes of the wagons hit the fence post and shattered into a thousand pieces. Debbie held the lines. Fred was trying desperately to catch up. Teresa was racing to get to Abbra, screaming for her to hang on. The wagons were heading straight for a stand of trees; there was no way out this time. Debbie could not stop them. Men from inside the fenced area began to run and jump the fence with a single bound without any thought of their own safety. They raced toward the frightened runaways. Ezra was there first and threw himself at the leaders; it was heartstopping to see. Then came Perry Jo and Mike Lowery. Everything came to a stop suddenly only a few strides from the stand of trees. A horrible accident had been prevented. I called to Fred to see if anyone needed medical help. He was smiling, of all things, and said, "Of course not." Abbra was still in the spring seat of the rear wagon. The seat had been bounced up off the holders, but the little girl had hung on. Teresa hurried up to the wagon and was met with, "Mama, are you all right?" Abbra was two years old.

I ran out of the pasture we were in to gather up all the belongings of the Shivers'. That was the least we could do. Many fell in behind me and we had everything quickly piled up and waiting for them.

The adventures of the day did not stop there. Three miles down the road, a locomotive came from behind us. We were traveling parallel to the tracks and knew the loud noise would raise havoc with some of the teams. Perry Jo and I knew for sure one team of mules would spook and run at any given moment, so we each rode our horses up close on each side of the team and squeezed them in between us so they could walk this one through without incident. One runaway always led to many more down the road. A good scout rider was priceless to the teamsters. They would ride alongside each wagon and were responsible for keeping an eye out for trouble spots and warn the drivers. Most of the scouts were a plus to the train but there were some that definitely were not. I know I made my share of errors when I scouted. I like to believe my help covered my mistakes in the long run.

Still our troubles didn't end. Soon after the last water stop Dorothy Allison took a bad fall from her horse as the animal stumbled. Dorothy was one of our staff riders. The horse fell on her, knocking her unconcious. We were all apprehensive as the ambulance took her away. Upon reaching camp, we learned Dorothy had a concussion, a chipped tooth, and double vision.

I will not say that to be a wagoneer you had to throw caution to the wind and do as you please, but people had to realize just what kind of a commitment we all made to do this in the first place. You do not just leave your homes, cars, modern day comforts, leases, friends, and loved ones just to trapse all over the countryside with total strangers—not without a lot of forethought and planning and inner commitment. Our injuries were taken very seriously; we cared about one another and ourselves very much. For a wagon train participant to leave the wagon train and call it quits, he had to be right at the end of every last hope of traveling on. We did not want to be martyred or looked at as superhuman beings. We started this journey with dedication, pride, and a hell of a lot of honor. This state and this nation was founded on total commitments; we felt them very seriously and lived them each and every mile that we made. Our forefathers were a tough bunch of people. We were not out to prove this, we just wanted to be a reminder to America and the citizens of Texas as to how they got their freedom and what it meant to use it. We wanted all the eyes to see what really made this a strong country, and what some of the settlers went through to get it as it is today and every day from this day forward.

If anyone can understand, then they might know why Dorothy returned to the train against the doctor's judgment a few days later. The saddle had to wait a spell, but she would travel in a wagon.

That night we stayed at the Perfection Land and Cattle Company. Not real conducive to the day, but a very pretty place. We were hosted to a wonderful meal, then went to bed early. The next day was to be thirty-two miles—and this time we were ready.

The twenty-fifth day of January will forever be carved in our minds. Magnolia, Texas, served us lunch with a warm reception and hospitality. They were glad to have us roll into their area. The camp jacks brought our shuttle buses out to give some of the teamsters in the wagons an opportunity to return to the old camp and bring forward their support vehicles to the new camp, just as we had done on the last long days' travel. Tragedy struck the wagon train. Pam Burchell of Newark, Texas caught the shuttle bus and died as a result of an accident while driving a friend's support vehicle forward. Like most of us, Pam had worked hard to be able to participate on the Texas Wagon Train. She left Sulphur Springs with us and traveled down through east Texas, out through the piney woods, over Livingston Reservoir, and in toward Tomball. At two-forty that afternoon, Pam had been taken from us. The last words she spoke to me were," Good morning, butterfly"—an expression of affection on her part.

The camp was rocked right down to our foundation. Then we realized exactly how the original settlers must have felt when they laid one of their own to rest by the roadway and had to roll out without them.

Sunday morning, Charles Oliver, the President of The Texas Wagon Train Association, spoke inside the circle of wagons. There were saddled horses ready with riders in silence and teamsters holding the lines. Mr. Oliver gave a brief statement of the passing of our lost wagoneer. Her wagon was still in the circle, but no horse was to pull that day. The little green wagon with the tongue toward the sky was almost ghostlike as we would pull around it to go on our way. Mr. Oliver also led us in a prayer. As his heartfelt words echoed across the wagons, we all shed tears, unashamed as we were truly pioneers now.

Another freedom came to mind that had been paid for with the spilling of blood. We had reached back and touched another time at that moment with the loss of a pioneer—be it 1986 or 1836, it is all the very same. A solemn pilgrimage pulled out of Tomball, marred by an accident, but determined to continue, for a memory will never die. Pam would make this journey as she had planned; we would not release her from our hearts.

Chapter Twelve

I had discovered, for me, that it was a real treat to be up around four-thirty every morning. It gave me a chance to see the camp come alive. One morning, I was making my way to the blue room when an obstruction got in my way.

Dark though it may have been, I spotted a skunk between myself and the blue room. We both saw one another about the same time. When one is traveling in the fashion we all were, it was best to look out for different critters at all times. You did not know where the next snake, tarantula, or skunk was to turn up. I tried to reason with my little friend by calling out "shoo-shoo" and "don't lose your temper." The animal could have been rabid for all I knew, but I didn't think so as it seemed as if it wanted away from me as I did it. Mr. Skunk did start to leave, but not far enough. I was still not close enough to the blue room to enter. I repeated myself and we were at the standoff stage. However, I was getting desperate, and he couldn't have cared less about my needs. Next, I just told him to leave me alone and tend to his family, whereupon the skunk dashed away—right under the blue room! Swell! I knew this wouldn't work. If I stepped up on the stairs and let the door slam as they did, he'd cut loose with that fragrance and there I'd be, following the wagon train a couple of miles back from that point to El Paso. Therefore, I turned and hiked way over to the other facility on the opposite side of the campground. Mr. Skunk won that round.

Chapter Thirteen

The winds hit us just outside Hempstead and never let go the rest of the day. I had traveled the total journey with the train and managed to keep my hat where it was supposed to be—except this day. The wind got to me three times. It is considered a weakness if one cannot keep one's hat on at all times in any kind of circumstances. It's rather like an old wive's tale. I also dropped my halter and lead line that I carried all the time; plus my gloves hit the ground twice. The wind was bad enough, but dismounting for any reason led to other problems. Getting back in the saddle wasn't always the easiest or safest maneuver; my mare was so sure that the entire train would go off and leave her whenever I got off. These trips to the ground that day where no different. To double the confusion for the animal, I had on enough clothing to make my mounting and dismounting a real struggle. Especially the blanket-robe I wore all the time during the cold weather. It was just an old brown blanket with a hole cut in the center where a sweaterneck piece was stitched into it to finish the appearance of the blanket nicely. On me the blanket hung to the ground; this garment always caught on some part of the saddle as I mounted. Lady moved whenever she felt my weight in the stirrup and I was always trying to unhook something, get a hold of her, and get us started in the right direction simultaneously. Meanwhile, the wagons and horses passed by and she wanted to go. The best kind of horse to have is one that will wait for the rider's command to move; not all of us had those.

Chapter Fourteen

The day we were in Hempstead, Texas, the space shuttle blew up, taking the lives of all seven crew members, including the first schoolteacher to qualify for the space program. There is no monoply on death, be it the new frontier or the old. The teacher from the space shuttle was to meet us down the road to tell our students on the wagon train about her adventures in space. They in turn, would share their stories of the train with her. The old and new had crossed trails again.

Our school on the wagon train was assembled before the wagons rolled out of Sulphur Springs. We started with twenty-seven students. One senior, Laurie Warner, would graduate from high school when we reached Ponder, Texas on June twenty-fifth. The students ranged from ages six to eighteen, and from kindergarten through the twelfth grade. They not only studied history as no other students had done before in modern-day times, but created history at the front of many historical places we passed along the trail. The teaching staff was three; Ms. Anita Pitchford, Ms. Susan Venus, and Mr. Randy Russell. With these three and not a large number of students, they did quite well, for a trouble spot was discovered early and corrected at that time. A great advantage.

Our school students took advantage of every field trip and historical spot in the entire state, I believe. It wasn't always easy for them either, as it meant early morning risings and long bus trips that lasted late into the night hours. In many cases this was to teach them about an event that took place more than a century ago. Some of the students still had chores involving the livestock when they returned to camp. It was my observation that if anyone took time to ask these students about a side trip they had taken, they sounded like a tour guide themselves when they returned. It didn't matter what they studied, whether it was a monument, a candy factory, or a wildlife reserve with an endangered species of nature's creations. They were a fabulous group of young people, and I loved them all. The teachers went way past the call of duty to get these kids an education on the wagon train trek. From the head schoolmarm, Ms. Anita, to Ms. Susan and Mr. Randy, they all rose to the occasion and brought the students passed the point of just everyday mundane lessons. My hat is off to all of them. I could not even begin to suggest anything but straight A's to them.

Chapter Fifteen

We crossed the Brazos River going into Brenham, and this, of course, could not be done without incident. Just because we were on a bridge instead of forging the river itself as our predecessors had done made no difference. The bridge had three separate places where shiny teethlike fittings stretched across its width. The surface of the fittings were smooth, but the teams and saddle horses had not seen anything of its kind before. Some of them shied to the left to escape the obstacle. The weight of the moving wagons would just push the teams across. The saddle horses reared and shied and whirled around to try to escape. Usually if one went across, the others would just follow without incident. It was the teams that created the biggest problem. Staff riders just dismounted and led them over the spot. The funniest crossing was Al Winder's wagon from Forth Worth. He had two Belgian horses in the hitch. The horse on the inside decided it was all right to cross, but only if the metal pieces were jumped. The other animal had already made up his mind that the metal pieces were not to be crossed at any length. Thus, the inside horse jumped high in the air, clearing the crossing by at least two feet. His teammate sat down like a dog and refused to make any effort to cross the metal monster. Between the force of the wagon going forward and the momentum of the jumping horse, the unwilling animal went across the obstacle without dignity or grace, being dragged in a sitting, resisting position. Laughter was the only response and we all enjoyed it.

Chapter Sixteen

As the wagons rolled out of camp toward Carmine, I decided to give Lady a day of rest, so I borrowed another horse and rode this day into a little town just off the main road with the rest of the train. Burton was the name of the community. Entering into town at our usual four-mile-an-hour pace, we were greeted by an old, comfortable little town, clean, with some ancient buildings that still house active businesses. The wagon train literally took up all of the room on their main street. We double lined the wagons and Burton, Texas came to a standstill for one hour. We had rolled through town and wound our way to the right down a small hill. Our water trucks were parked previous to our arrival. Everyone began to get out of their wagons to care for the stock. Riders dismounted. Then businessmen, in their suits walked amongst us to served drinks, both cold and hot. The girlscouts came by with bags of cookies that had been put together lovingly for the wagoneers. I would say everyone of the six hundred citizens of the town were sitting or standing somewhere to see the wagon train. Old timers leaned back in their chairs against store fronts to watch and swap stories of when *they* drove a team or their fathers and mothers did. It was a treat for them and it was sure a treat for the wagoneers. Another little town in Texas had shown the hospitality that the southern part of this nation is so famous for. Garry mounted his horse, threw back his head and another "wagons-ho!" put big smiles on the townsfolks' faces as the historic journey walked further into history. Just outside of Burton, the horse I had borrowed showed signs of not being quite right. I let him fall back if he wanted and take a slower pace. It wasn't·long before the back of the last wagon was pulling away from us. I didn't know what was wrong, but I dismounted and led the horse to see if relieving him of my weight would help. By this time, we were way behind the train. Bert Payne, one of the staff riders, fell back with me to see if I needed help. I had told many of the riders and drivers as they passed to send the vet when they saw him. Bert said he would walk with me until help arrived. Vickie Barrett drove by but had no room in her trailer for the horse. She took my saddle to lighten the load a bit more. Bert and I walked on. We both had on boots that were not made for walking. Such is life on the trail. We walked about four miles. An empty horse trailer came by from the wagon train. I loaded that horse and ran out into the highway, stoppng traffic to be able to catch the shuttle bus returning to the last camp to get Ms. Susan's rig and Lady. I must add, the drivers of all the vehicles were very good about the holdup and most patient with me and my helpers. Bert and I were only about one-half mile from the new camp. Bert mounted up again to ride on into camp and I realized that chivalry did live and breathe on the wagon train.

Chapter Seventeen

Our ride into Giddings found us with more runaways and injuries. Plus I started learning how to drive a team. Miss Hazel said I could ride with her. About four miles into the day, she said it was about time I learned to drive that outfit. So with her careful, wise guidance, I began my driving lessons. For Miss Hazel, it was old hat, as she had had a set of lines in her hands for seventy-five years of her seventy-eight. It has always been my experience, if you want to know anything about anything, go find someone that has done it for about fifty years or so. They are your teachers. Leo Miller, driver of the Copenhagen/Skoal, Billy Bob's wagon, had his daughter, Carol, traveling with him. They had been separated for thirty-five years. Her search for him had brought her to the wagon train. We were all happy for both of them, and enjoyed seeing them travel together on the train. This day she had borrowed a horse to ride and it became frightened during a runaway. In fact, five teams at once spooked and ran. Carol's horse fell, crushing her leg beneath it on the pavement. She was rushed to the hospital in Austin. Her knee had been shattered and the ankle was destroyed. Seven months later, the injury had not healed, and Leo told me the foot may have to come off. A very sad day for us all, but father and daughter had found one another.

Chapter Eighteen

When the wagon train pulled up in front of the community center in McDade, it was a toss up again as to who was most glad who was there. Refreshments were served and the senior citizens of the area were sitting in a semicircle in front of the center. I walked over to talk to each of them. As it had been throughout the journey, the old people would reach out and touch and hang on. They would tell us, "Do not give up your journey, stay with it." All of this encouragement did not fall on closed ears. It was the kind of spirit that kept the train going and we were very appreciative that we had such words along the way from people that knew what it took to keep the wagon train going. I wish I could remember all of the names of our senior welcomers in McDade, but I don't. It did not occur to me to get them on paper. Some of them had lived in the area since they arrived there in covered wagons many years ago. They wished us all well as we rolled out of sight. We caught our breath a time or two when we waved and they returned it with a smile and a handkerchief flowing in the breeze after they wiped their eyes.

Chapter Nineteen

Finally, Austin—our first big city! We had heard so many rumors about Austin. On this day we would camp on a race track and enjoy alligator stew. The dish was not really enjoyed by all, but I thought it was good. Bobby came to see me and made the two days he was with me much better. When I was making the plans for this journey, I made many lists of necessary items I would need and planned very carefully what to bring on a light scale, versus the unneeded things we women tend to pack along. I can be just as guilty as any other female at committing this unwelcomed error. At the same time, I overlooked one major fact. I missed my husband more than I thought was possible. As previously mentioned, we had only just married when the idea of the wagon train was released. I was so wrapped up in getting ready for over a year, the thought of being without him occurred to me of course, but the actuality of it did not. I can only say I adjusted to being without Bobby but I never got used to it. I looked forward to his visits with great excitement. He would sit for hours as I told him of the adventures on the trail. He was my most attentive audience and always took the tales back to our friends and family in Fort Worth. Some of the marriages were under a great strain while the wagons rolled. I was not the only person traveling without my mate. It takes a very strong person to go along with his or her partner taking off and leaving them for six months. I could not have done it without my husband's total support both financially and mentally. He allowed me to do what I wanted to do with my life; he allowed me to have a dream and approved of me making it come true. I will put it in print. Thank you, Bobby Stepp. I love you for just being you and letting me be me.

Chapter Twenty

Just outside of Austin, we crossed the first five hundred mile marker. This was a major crossing for us. We had lived with so many negative words from the public that we were not going to stay on the road for two days, let alone five hundred miles.

Then a bad message reached our ears. We were not going to be able to circle the capitol building. A change of plans followed that statement; thirty wagons were going to be "allowed to circle." A lot of comments were voiced with that silly statement. A short while later it was back to the not being able to circle again. I do not know where this changing of minds came from. It became a very confusing issue from the wagoneer's viewpoint. The last statement we heard may have been hearsay, but we liked it the best: all of the wagons would roll around the capitol or none! It appeared that the strong roots of this pilgrimage began to show through. Everyone was going, the whole damn bunch, and it felt like a battle won.

Mother nature played a dirty trick, however. We were rained on worse than we had been since leaving Sulphur Springs one month and one day earlier. I rode beside Suzanne Whitfield's one-horse covered wagon. Pat Schmidt was with her and we began to laugh hysterically. Here we were in the middle of a rain storm trying desperately to stay dry and vowing this was the best time we had had in our entire lives. We wondered how anyone could possibly think we were crazy. This may not sound funny to a lot of people but it sure struck us that way and still does.

Chapter Twenty-One

By now, I was sleeping in the back of Susan Venus' horse trailer. Rolling my bedroll out on a couple of bales of hay each night, I was most comfortable. There was a plastic tarp on the sides of the trailer to keep out most of the foul weather, but this time the weather was worse than foul. Traveling seven miles that day brought us into camp early. The driving rain emptied the campgrounds quickly and I hurried into my "Horsetrailer Hilton" to take shelter. Much to my chagrin, the "Hilton" leaked. I managed to find a small dry spot and slept that night in a half-sitting, half-lying position—not very conducive to sound sleeping. Our next day was the day we were to circle the capitol. Our attitudes were high and a rainstorm was not about to slow us down. I always had invitations to quarter in other camps to get away from the elements of the bad weather, but I was not suffering, therefore I chose to keep my area in the "Horsetrailer Hilton." Bobby had left early that day. I slept with the sound of the rain dancing across the trailer top and singing me into a restless long night.

The plans to take the wagon train and circle the capitol building had been changed so often that I truly did not believe we could do it until that morning when all of the teams strained in the harnesses and pulled with every ounce of strength they had to get the wagons out of the mudhole they were in. God, what a sight! Wagon after wagon came up out of the muck onto the pavement. I do not know what the trouble was with all of us circling the capitol, but rumors were flying. One stuck in my mind. It may never have been said, but I don't know. However, rumor had it that the wagoneers just were not serious about this journey. Let me insert right here: as I sat there on my horse watching each of those wagons being pulled out of the mud, I had tears of pride and I wasn't alone. With all of the combined force that each human being and head of stock could father, the wagons arose from that black land mud. Whoops and hollers, tears and laughter, we all knew that we had reached a milestone. With lumps of pride in our throats and inherited dignity within our souls, we wrote yet another page in history and rolled on into the heart of Austin to circle the capitol building.

What a sight to see, that old stately building with many people standing by it, in it, and around it—surrounded by trees and other greenery and being circled by the Texas Wagon Train. We echoed our feelings of pride, shouted our hellos to the building tops, and waved as if we would not see another day. The past reached the present riding straight into the future. Our hearts were so filled with a great accomplishment. From way up to the many stories above our heads came the same exuberant waving as was on the ground. Pulling away from the capitol, we looked back to see the rest of the train make that last turn and come straight away from the building down off the hill. Many were still along the streets welcoming us and reaching out. We had done it and were on the greatest high there is: self-dedication and inner pride.

When we arrived in camp and took care of the livestock, Quentin McGown, our business manager, read a proclamation the capitol had made that day and a second from the governor. He read loud and clear. The words were heard throughout camp. Austin, for us, had been a success despite what anyone had or had not said; let that lay to rest. The Texas Wagon Train was strong in spirit and determined in mind. It was from this day forward I started to write my heartfelt words in the form of poems. My first piece of work was very well received:

> If you want to know your freedoms,
> Feel the breeze upon your back,
> Come travel with the pioneers,
> Your thoughts can wander back
>
> To a century ago
> With teams a pulling on,
> Children laughing, playing, crying
> Watched over by their moms.
>
> No pavement did they follow
> Or welcomes they did get,
> Just miles and miles of Texas
> And the sun as it did set.
>
> They gave their blood for freedoms,
> Worked hard to form this land,
> The Lone Star state was built,
> Through a woman and a man.
>
> Their graves have long been covered
> From snow, and sleet, and rain
> Brought back to be remembered
> By the Texas Wagon Train.

Chapter Twenty-two

Since our journey began, we always traveled toward the south; therefore, the weather was not real bad for us. Actually, our biggest enemy was heat. Unseasonable weather caused us to be in the heat while the livestock still had all of their winter coats. This caused the wagon train to lose another head of stock the day we came around the capitol. We were once again saddened by the loss as the animals were our only way of making this journey. A lot of wagoneers considered the stock a part of their families. This comparison can be transferred back to a century ago, also. For without the livestock, our original settlers could not find their promised lands. We lived with these comparisons daily.

Rolling into Lockhart found us trying to handle runaways again. One of the teams of mules decided it was much quicker to run into camp way ahead of everyone else and be there hours earlier than just to go with the flow. We had some very good staff outriders and volunteers helping whenever it was necessary—not for gain, but because they were needed. Wet weather had caused the roads to be slick. A few of the wagons slipped and skidded into the entrance. Careful guiding hands brought them through without incident, but it didn't prevent gasps. Nelda French and I caught the bus to the showers; it was good to smell better than one's horse again. A street dance was held in our honor, slanted street surface with potholes and all! A real dancer could add a few new steps while trying to get around some of the dance floors we had to use during this journey.

J. R. Newton was one of our campjacks. This is a position filled by a man that must tolerate the foul attitudes of many tired people every day just to keep the camps moving smoothly and see that everyone is settled in for the night without too many complaints on a daily basis. It was always my opinion that he was a priceless man that overworked himself to the point of sheer exhaustion and kept going. No amount of praise or salary could really reward J. R. enough as far as this wagoneer could see. On this day, J. R. lost a battle with a trailer jack when it hit him in the jaw. His expert help had to go on without sound for a while.

Chapter Twenty-three

On the sixth of February, we rolled on to Luling. I rode with Miss Hazel that day as Lady had a runny nose and was on medication. Miss Hazel continued to teach me the points of driving a team. She told me first off what to do if a team ever runs away. Mainly the driver should stay calm. I thought to myself, *Sure, no problem. If this team or any other team got to running, it's easy to think calm. After all, you only have your life to lose as these maniacs race down an Interstate highway or a back country road, where the barbed wire can slash skin to ribbons in a split second. No problem.*

Little did I know this advice would be used quicker than I ever thought. Miss Hazel climbed to the back of the wagon to take a short nap back behind two spring seats and other belongings in the wagon. It was necessary to crawl on one's prayer bones to get to the back of the wagon. The seats sat so high it was easier to go under. No sooner had Miss Hazel laid down to rest when the ultimate test hit full force. A palomino horse raced by us like the wind, running at full speed in fright, a saddle hanging beneath its belly, and two riders in hot pursuit of the frightened animal. The team of mules I was driving spooked and bolted around the lead wagon. We were on our way down the middle of the road. I stood up and grabbed two hands full of lines wrapping each line twice and began to talk to those two mules in the most calm manner I have ever talked to anything in my whole life. While in such an excited state of mind. I could just hear Miss Hazel's words as she was telling me earlier about how important the calm attitude was. I eased that brake on, and those mules slowed to a walk in no time. It was just as we were back in the right place. I looked over my shoulder and Miss Hazel was scrambling up the floorboards as fast as she could on her hands and knees to get to the lines. She jumped up beside me with her bonnet on at an odd angle, what with the rough trip to the front. She took one look at me and said, "Land sakes, Donna, you done good." I was shaking like a leaf, but she had missed that part. I was just lucky and Miss Hazel had given me very good advice on what to do.

We noticed other wagons had runaways also. Wagons were all over the place. The palomino had spooked all of them. Worst of all, the Grandy sponsored wagon, driven by Travis Reeves and his wife Alene, was upside down in the middle of the highway. My heart sank as I looked out back down the line and saw the wagon lying on its side; the mules were thrashing on the roadway. We could not do a thing for them, as the team we had was very nervous and had to be held tightly to prevent them from running again. Travis and Alene are Garry's aunt and uncle.

Garry raced back to the overturned wagon. All of the available riders helped without getting in the way of the downed wagon. I learned later Alene was in the back of the wagon and automatically threw up her arms to protect herself from the flying seats and other articles in the wagon as it went over. Travis was thrown out of the front seat on top of the mules thrashing on the ground. He was uninjured; Alene had escaped with a bad bruise on her left leg. When Travis hurried back to call to his wife as she lay inside the wagon, she called to him the only thing she could think of: "Travis, get the camera." That is exactly what he did. Mr. Reeves is seventy and Mrs. Reeves is sixty-six. God had helped a great deal with this accident and we knew it. The palomino had been stopped but just as the riders got to him, he stepped through one of the loose stirrups and broke his leg nearly off. He was destroyed immediately. We had suffered another loss.

The mayor of Luling, Bill Hooper, was in camp to greet us personally when the wagons rolled in. We would thank him as we went on our way to tend to the stock.

The next day, Miss Hazel was ill, so I was asked to drive her wagon. She was going to tough it out and ride in the wagon. Her determination was no worse than anyone else on this outfit. Linda Rayshell rode with me. We bundled Miss Hazel up and went on our way toward a very historic town in Texas, Gonzales. Cloudy skies and cool weather covered us all day. As soon as we turned to go into the campground, the sun shown on the lead wagon only. We were being watched over again.

Gonzales is the sight of a very brief battle of one hundred fifty-one years before. On the sight where our camp was set up, a battle took place in 1835 that lasted just a few minutes. Only one shot was fired from a cannon. The same cannon was still in the town, also in working order. Later that evening during the program for the wagoneers, the cannon was fired for us for the first time since 1835. Gonzales was where the famous "Come And Get It" battle was fought. There, the townsfolk fought the Mexican army off with this small cannon to keep their town. When we thought about the time and history involved around this little cannon, it was an emotional group of wagoneers that heard the cannon roar. They had done this just for us and we knew and felt it. That small cannon had been lost at the bottom of the creek bed for a century, found, and restored to its original look in 1936. It is housed in Gonzales but displayed throughout Texas from time to time.

These types of reminders from last century helped the pioneers of the eighties to hold onto the faith that we would make this journey all the way to Fort Worth. Our spirits were lifted tremendously.

Chapter Twenty-four

Lady was sick with the flu—not real bad, but I wanted to keep her in top shape so I either rode in a wagon or drove a team for about a week. I was not alone with my situation of having only one mount with me on the trip. We would borrow a mount or hop a wagon to keep going down the road. My personal commitment would not allow me to miss a traveling day unless a leg or an arm was broke—then again, I'm not sure about that either.

One day I rode with Suzanne Whitfield and Pat Schmidt in the back of Suzanne's wagon. The day was very cold plus the wind was blowing. I was as bundled as I could get. Climbing in the wagon, I fell into the back head first and became lodged upside down without the balance to right myself. It took both of the girls to upright me again. When we circled the wagons for the lunch stop, Suzanne drove the wagon around into position away from the wind, I'd tucked myself in and was sitting on two very thick cushions. My viewpoint was only straight ahead so I missed the turn down a steep dip. The horse pulled suddenly and jerked the wagon, dumping me upside down once again. I just started to laugh. Pat grabbed what she thought was my hand to keep me balanced and Suzanne guided us into parking position not realizing I was in need of her assistance again. What Pat actually had a strong grip on was my foot. I was bundled up to much to tell what end was what and I could not stop laughing long enough to tell them. Everyone knows you cannot laugh and do anything at the same time. Glyn Pearce from the WBAP wagon came running to see how so much laughter could escape a tiny wagon. We could not explain. One had to be there to even believe it or appreciate it.

Chapter Twenty-five

Cuero found us once again in the cold, cold wind. I drew my bales of hay around me closer to ward off the chill. I knew if I was dry I would be warm. The idea worked well and I thought I was better off than those with butane tanks that had run out and thought they were freezing to death.

A large group of us took advantage of the tour bus that was made available for those wanting to learn about this town and a little bit about the roots of Cuero and its background. Some of the most magnificent architecture I have ever seen from a century ago was to greet us.

Kenny and Carol Taylor found a horse around Cuero that was not being taken care of properly. They purchased the animal from someone out in the surrounding country, named him Cuero, and a new participant was added to the population of the train. He ended up being one of the top horses on the trip and a real pioneer.

Chapter Twenty-six

The newspaper was always there whenever we stopped. It was not the easiest thing along the trail when we were hot, or cold, or tired, or whatever the case may be, to say the most pleasant things. But I will add, most of our words were always positive. We really believed the wagon train was going all the way to the stockyards in Forth Worth by July 3. We believed it because we knew our strengths and weaknesses. The rest of the opinions did not count in our eyes.

Martha Burns, who was most instrumental and active getting us on our tour around Cuero, looked totally out of place amongst wagon train people dressed in our wagon train clothing of the 1800s. However, she was a trouper beyond belief. She had spent the day with us still looking like she stepped out of a fashion magazine. She asked me to share a few words with the local reporter. I agreed and she insisted on getting my plate of food from the serving line and bringing it to me. I was embarrassed to have this lovely lady do such a thing for me in my usual wagon train dirt. Matt Williams of Donaldson, Arkansas was being interviewed by the reporter whose name was Jackie. Jackie started to ask me some questions. I asked to continue with my meal as I was more relaxed doing something. I started to talk about my feelings. I told her that the trip meant many things, most of them quite simply patriotic. I have strong feelings about America and Texas in particular. I wasn't paying attention to Jackie and Martha after I got started, but I glanced up at a given point to look toward the two ladies; they both had tears flowing. I had come to understand these tears represented pride, honor, and respect for us wagoneers for our part in accomplishing an old-fashioned venture in a modern day world.

Chapter Twenty-seven

I had a real scare in the middle of one night when Lady was kicked by one of the other horses she was tied near. I rushed to the vet's, and he came quickly, as he always did. Dr. Ken gave her a shot to calm her and relax the muscles. It looked as if the leg was broken; she would have to remain sedated until she could be transported to another vet the next day. The next morning, her leg still looked bad so the vet took her on up to the next camp. I borrowed another horse to ride and waited for word about my pal. It was evening before I saw the mare again; her leg had lost all of the swelling. Dr. Ken and I both agreed it was another unusual incident, but we were not going to question it.

Chapter Twenty-eight

Our arrival into Goliad, Texas was just like it would have been one hundred fifty years ago if we would have come in right behind Santa Anna's troops that had just massacred Colonel Fanin's company of soldiers. It was a happy occasion for us but the church bells began to ring, creating an eerie feeling. The very same bells had rung the day of the massacre. We could not escape the tears as we were touched in a very special way. We paraded around the town square and most of the townspeople were there to greet us, waving their handkerchiefs. The majority of the population are of Mexican descent, so it was very easy to see into the last century, again, to when Texas was shedding so much blood before being admitted into the union.

As we passed through a lot of the towns of Texas, along the trail, the people of the communities would dress in costumes of the 1800s to welcome us. Goliad sure represented the theme well.

That little town still had the original hanging tree in front of the courthouse in the town square. It was old and leaning. Some of the limbs reached down and touched the ground, but it was still complete and growing. Just like the wagon train, it was a symbol all the way from last century.

The next morning, the fog was about two feet thick on the ground. Rolling out of camp on the roadway south just outside of Goliad, we passed the oldest presidio in the nation, the oldest fort in America that still stands today, exactly as it did when Colonel Fanin's men were quartered there 150 years ago. It actually dates back to the 1700s, when Goliad was first settled. Our covered wagon train rolled past the Presidio La Bahia in the quiet of that Sunday morning; the canvas covered transports moved slowly with teams walking into the quiet morning air. Then the bells rang. Someone had gone to the belfry and, by hand, was sending us a message of blessings. We could not help but catch our breaths. Turning our glance toward the old fort, we saw a statue of a woman holding a chained dead child, representing the Goliad massacre of 1836.

Chapter Twenty-nine

My celebration of Valentine's Day was with a very bad case of the flu. We were down in south Texas. I missed my husband on this special day for loved ones to spend together. Now this would make you feel sorry for yourself, believe me. We were all beginning to miss the folks back home. We had one another, but it was not the same as being with a family member that you loved.

The attitudes of the wagoneers came and went in a wave like that of the oceans. We were all melancholy, lonesome and excited all at the same time about a coming event. I believe this is why we understood one another so well. Miss Hazel had the flu and stayed in camp at the nurse's house. Everyone's campsite was called their house. Doug Medlin had the flu and should have been resting but wouldn't give in to it. My voice was beginning to fade but that was no great loss. The wagon train's first three-night layover was in Kingsville, so I thought if I could just hold in there until we arrived, I could get three good nights' sleep and make it fine. I was close to being right. I was so sick and worn out from my fight with the flu, by the time we made Kingsville, I didn't care if I lived or died. Mark Morton took Lady and told me not to give her a second thought. He would water and feed her so I could rest. Mark was a life saver. He kept his word and I got lots of much needed rest. We had corrals and box stalls for the livestock, making the layover there good for everyone. I was not alone with the illness. It was the type of flu that worked its way through the wagon train participants with brutality, showing no mercy. Eventually everyone had the misfortune of having it.

Chapter Thirty

Arriving in Kingsville was another major turning point for us. This was our southernmost point of travel in the state.

Most of the wagoneers were enjoying high spirits with this accomplishment. Dr. Ken, who always seemed to enjoy a practical joke, had bought a live-looking mouse. He would sneak up to an unprepared wagoneer and lay it down. I was riding with O. C. Horn from Quitman, Texas when Dr. Ken chose to lay the little critter right down beside me. Naturally it caught me unaware and I think I remember yelling something unkind to him, much to his enjoyment.

Seeing the famous King Ranch was a sight we all had looked forward to. In fact, the original plans were to stay on the ranch. This idea was changed but we were always up against these changes throughout the journey. The wagoneers were quartered in a park and were able to take a tour bus to the ranch if we so desired. I went with other participants in a truck from camp and made the loop around the tour area twice. On the second round, we were approached by one of the hands from the ranch to stop the truck and help give a hand to the horsemen driving a small herd of cattle up to the main training barn to work out a few head of horses that were being trained to cut cattle. I jumped out first and considered it a real privilege to be a "hand" on the King Ranch, even if only for a few minutes. The trainers and handlers put on an exhibition for the wagoneers about training cutting horses.

It was the dead of winter by this time, the eighteenth of February. The temperature was ninety-eight degrees. Our main concern was for the stock, three days off and coupled with their heavy winter coats still on. We wanted to leave town early, but the fog was so thick it delayed our departure for over an hour. I had gone to the nurse to get some medicine for my cough and flu. My voice was nonexistent; everybody asked me questions just so they could hear me not answer them. Cute folks!

All of the teams were in harness. The saddle horses walked around slowly as the wagoneers were ready, but the fog just clung to the area. Finally word was given. Garry's "wagons ho!" echoed and we left camp almost at a run. All of the animals had become anxious; they did not understand waiting while all geared up, and instinct told them it was past time to roll.

Courtney Hall's team started out of turn with the driver in the back of the wagon. A quick move from one of the staff members saved their bacon. I rode scout for O. C. Horn that day and his two big draft mares took off like bats out of hell. My mare and I stayed right beside the wagon lopping alongside to keep up. Many people were lined along the street. I rode out behind them through the trees to keep from pushing them out of the way and causing any injury. The wagoneers hollered and whooped. We must have looked like a wild west show thundering out of town.

Right after leaving camp, we passed a school with at least fifteen hundred students of all ages waiting for us to come by. Every one of them had a red kerchief tied around his neck. They must have bought every bandana in the county to get that many, God love them. They also held handmade Texas flags, waving them with a lot of pride shining in their little faces. Right past the school, the Courtney Hall wagon in front of Mr. Horn's wagon had one of their mules fall right down on the pavement. The mule jumped up apparently unhurt, but it looked like it was going to be one of those days for that outfit.

Later the temperature became almost overbearing. One of Mr. Horn's mares overheated. Doctor Ken took the horse in. In fact, he took the team. Peggy White, head of the Dairy Queen outfit, offered Mr. Horn her mules to get his wagon to the lunch stop. Then he had to see what the next choice was. Horn's wagon had fallen back about a mile or two before he was rehooked and ready to roll again. I loaded Lady and rode on into camp with Chris Red Cloud. Horn's wagon was without horsepower after the lunch stop and needed a transport trailer to haul the wagon on into camp. Courtney Hall pulled in and I asked him if he could go out and pick up Mr. Horn. The wagon train had taken a different route than the support vehicles. Therefore, he did not understand the way out I offered to direct him. Courtney was very pleased to be of help, but I missed the turn and managed to get us about fifteen miles out in the wrong direction. I don't think I will ever forget how patient Courtney was with my incorrectness. Anyone that knows the man will surely get a big laugh out of this little story, as Courtney Hall was not known for his easy nature. We eventually found Mr. Horn patiently waiting in the heat alongside the farm road and brought the wagon into camp.

Chapter Thirty-one

Our journey took us into San Diego, and what a welcome that community gave us. San Diego will always be remembered as the little town with the giant welcoming heart. From the old to the young, they welcomed us with open arms and big smiles. The students gave us all of their best school cheers complete with cheerleaders. Again, the senior citizens were sitting under a big open tent to shade them. We called out to those special people and, true to every other elderly group we had passed, these ladies and gentlemen came to life as I know they had not done in years. It was such a sight. The tears flowed as the cheering continued. I made a comment that someone should have had the foresight to take a picture of the senior citizens jumping into the air if no other shot was taken in the whole town. Their enthusiasm was wonderful. I was riding scout for the Horn wagon going into town. Courtney Hall was right in front of this wagon's team. I dropped one of my reins just as someone from the streetside caught Horn's attention. Horn's wagon ran right into the Hall wagon as

Horn had missed the stop signal that I should have given, but missed when I dropped a rein. Lady became nervous so I dismounted to retrieve it. Then, Apache Barrett's team, directly behind Horn, was having a problem so I hurried back to help him. As I turned to mount up, my mare whirled around and stepped on my right foot. Her spiked shoes ground into my foot and it felt like it was broken. The pain was like fire. Someone ran and got ice to pack on it quickly and a police car was their immediately. The officers carried me to their car and drove me on to the next camp. We were only about two miles away but I was going to miss the ceremony at the town square. I was told later it was one of the best, as was always the truth with small towns.

Later that evening, Carol Taylor took me back to the hospital in Alice to have the foot x-rayed. It was not broken, just bruised. I was luckier than our stage man; just as I returned to camp, he fell off of the stage and broke his foot. He always wanted to return to the wagon train and tried everything he could to do so, but the end of the trail came before Frank could return. He and his wife were missed by many. They were real troupers and a very pleasant couple.

We had the first of many wagoneer talent shows in San Diego. I shared the first poem I had written the day we circled the capitol building. Suzanne Whitfield sang "The Alamo" as we had never heard her sing before. It was fabulous. J. W. Jines played his french harp. Mark, our Purina Feed truckdriver gave us a new song, "The Blue Room Song," a very funny song about getting caught in the blue room when Garry hollered "wagons ho!" I could relate to the piece as that had happened to me once. The young people that worked for Cody Marketing, our official sourvenir vendors, sang a song called "Friends" that put a chill throughout everyone. Many joined in our impromptu shows that always provided close fellowship.

The next morning, we left camp. There was a chill in the air. These temperture changes would not give relief to the wagoneers with flu or colds. Everyone was aware of this and looked out for one another to be sure no animals were left unattended because of an ailing flu-struck owner. Once again the great comradery was there in full scale.

I rode most of the day going into Freer, but my foot was so swollen I had to back off just four miles out of camp. I loaded Lady in one of the camp's empty trailers passing by and hopped a wagon. I went to get her as soon as we pulled into camp. She had made the trip fine; my saddle had not. I was a little angry, to put it tactfully. A good saddle that fits your needs and is broken in perfectly cannot be replaced, especially in the middle of a three-thousand-mile horseback ride. The saddle was eventually replaced with a new one by the person that was responsible for it when it disappeared. The new one was not the quality mine had been and I ultimately sold it at the auction we had in the stock yards at the end of the trail.

Chapter Thirty-two

A full moon brought the worst of everything out. This observation was not just for the people. The livestock always broke loose more during a full moon than any other time of the month and more of our injuries occurred at this time also. Not everyone believed in the moon and star happenings, however it did get to the point where more paid attention. Non-believers took precautions. Serious injuries coupled with tempers flared up the worst at these times. I had words with a troublemaker about camp during a full moon. I wasn't very proud of myself for the quick exchange even though the problem stopped. But I had always wished I had been a bit more diplomatic about the matter.

Chapter Thirty-three

Many photos were taken along the trail as we rolled further into history. I kidded Jan one day about her being responsible for putting the Kodak film industry back in the black by following through with her idea of taking a wagon train all around Texas. I had hoped she had made arrangements for residuals. All of the onlookers, as the train passed them, seemed to find the entire train awesome, but of course they had their favorites too. On many occasions, we wished we could see some of the shots they took. Luckily, from time to time these welcomed photographers would make a point to catch us on the road and give us a photo they had captured. Such was the case of the reigning Miss Teen Texas. She took a shot of me sitting on my mare up on a hill as I watched the train pass by me below. We never grew tired of watching all of those covered wagons pass and took every opportunity to watch. Cathy Cubs had her mother deliver the photo and I was most appreciative. This was to happen again down the trail with other photographers, not only to me but to each of us and will always be grateful to those people for making our journey better because of their caring.

Chapter Thirty-four

Just outside of San Antonio we lost another horse due to a trailer accident. It was sad, and we all felt it, for this horse was responsible for leading us into the wagon train circle every night as we entered our next campsite. The horse had been ridden by the campjack, J. R. Newton.

The wagoneers seemed to be in a wave of turmoil for the past few days. Arguments would occur between folks that just did not have cross words. Every gathering has its people who find it necessary to verbalize their unrestful feelings. This wagon train was the same as the original settlers train must have been, I'm sure. We had our disagreements, then it was back to helping one another again. Attitudes would adjust, then the trouble would settle down. Just before leaving camp to go into San Antonio, I was approached by one of the wives of the train and accused of taking her bridle and tie down. She was going to ride this day even though the gear was missing. She was absolutely sure about my stealing her belongings. This was a serious accusation and I stood and listened to her get it all out of her system as she screamed at the top of her lungs in the middle of camp. I did not take her gear. Trying to tell her this was fruitless, and I just walked away. However, she went running to her husband and two of her neighbors to let them know I was a thief. I was leading a horse across camp at the same time and chose to let the women rant and rave. This is not to say I didn't think about pulling her hair out of her head, as she deserved. I was angry enough to do it. However, the act wouldn't shut her up or find the missing gear. I was forced to walk back near her quarters on my return trip across camp. I remember almost cringing at the act. I cut a wide berth and she came at me again. She approached me and said she had found the missing gear and was wrong to have accused me. I felt like yelling back at her and asking if she could go out and scream her apologies at the top of her lungs to the people who had overheard her in the first place. But I didn't. I accepted, and asked that she give me some space and just let the matter lay. She always remained ugly to me from that day forward.

My thoughts were we must pull together stronger. This wagon train was going to Forth Worth if it took every ounce of self-discipline we could gather amongst us.

Chapter Thirty-five

Kay Lightfoot, from Lucy, Tennessee, and I put an honor guard together, for there was an interest among the wagoneers to post the flags of the states representing each state on the train. We had families from thirty states riding with us. Appropriately, these folks needed recognition. We practiced twice but the wind blew so hard the volunteers didn't get a chance to enjoy their efforts.

Chapter Thirty-six

I looked forward to seeing San Antonio more than any other part of the journey, mainly because I had never had the privilege of seeing the Alamo and the surrounding area. This was the roots of Texas, the foundation of this state. I could feel the presence of those that came before us more strongly here than anywhere else on the trail. At the same time the wagon train was in San Antonio, the actual battle between Colonel Travis and Santa Anna was raging, one hundred fifty years before. Most Americans study about the Alamo in history books and write reports throughout their years in school. The wagon train was camped on the grounds near the sight and walking in the very same footsteps of the brave soldiers, the volunteers if you will, that came before us. If you think about it, we were a handful of volunteers from Texas and other states. We had come to bow our heads and give our thanks.

Leaving Hidden Valley in south San Antonio to camp at the Freeman Coliseum for two nights started a day of adventure and three days of action we would never forget.

Hidden Valley had hosted us very well and we were most comfortable in the tree-surrounded park. While there on the creekbanks, the usual question was asked of us. Kenny Taylor answered better than anyone. The question of course was: "Is this train going to make it to Forth Worth?" Kenny looked right into the camera and told every listener in the viewing audience, "Yes. We're going to make it. In fact, my friend, you tell everybody to put their suits on, brush the moss off their teeth, and meet us at Main and Exchange in Forth Worth because we'll be there July third!" I don't know how the viewers liked the answer, but we did. It was just like we were fighting our own battle. With damn little support, we had no doubts whatsoever. Give up was not in our vocabulary.

As we rolled out of Hidden Valley, we were growing in numbers at this point. The wagon train always picked up a lot of wagons and riders just outside of the major cities or popular spots. Some would join at a point not far from homes, travel during their vacations or whatever time they had allotted, then go home. On this particular morning, one of the new teams of mules chose not to follow the rest of the pack. They took out through a plowed pasture as if it were not there. I saw them and spurred my mare to help. Greg Simmons, one of the staff outriders, went racing after them too, so I yielded to him. Another horse threw a shoe and trying to find it on the gravel road to have it reset at the waterstop was impossible. We had rolled out of camp very shorthanded of staff, due to sick horses and flu amongst the wagoneers. Many of the live-stock was just worn out and needed extra time off. In light of this, every rider that was qualified to help was needed.

Two miles out of camp, I looked over my shoulder back down the train, as was a practice in case someone behind needed aid. I noticed the McCrosson Boys' Ranch outfit from Sioux Falls, South Dakota, was loping to catch up. Lady and I were once again scouting for the Horn wagon. This wagon was seven wagons ahead of the McCrosson Boys' Ranch. For some reason they had fallen back about one hundred yards. It took me just a short time to see that McCrossons' was not just catching up. It was another runaway. I yelled to everyone to stop their teams quickly. My thoughts were to give the driver, Walt Schaffer, a clear shot of going wherever he could to get control of the runaway. Four big Belgians were in the hitch. Walt had the brakes locked, the wheels were smoking, and the seven wagons in front of him stopped with nervous teams prancing. Horn's wagon and the next two all waited for whatever was going to happen. Walt held the team on the roadway. When a team is running in fright there isn't really anything anyone can do to stop them. The movies always show riders catching up with runaways and stopping them. This can only be done by a very experienced stunt rider. We were fresh out of such riders. I urged the mare toward them around Horn's wagon and was told later I uttered the famous "Oh shit" again. To see animals of this size and power running in fright and knowing you are completely helpless is a sick feeling. I knew the teacher was in the wagon with all the boys, as they held their school while traveling down the road. Counting the driver, about nine people were in that wagon. As I came up the road toward them, the wagon and team veered off the road to the left, hooking the tongue of the wagon in a six foot cyclone fence and ripping it out of the ground as if it were paper. Walt still held the lines; then the tongue snapped in two. The lead horses had fallen down and been run over by the wheel team when the tongue broke. The wagon also went over the top of the downed animals. Walt hung on and the lines in his hands were stretched as far as they were going to, he continued to hang on but the force of the taunt lines captapulted the driver out of the wagon onto the ground. Everything had stopped as suddenly as it had begun. I raced to them calling to see if there was need for a medic. Walt was getting up looking for his glasses. He assured me all was well with the people. I whirled around to go get Doug Medlin. I looked up the line and the wagons were spread out with gaps in between, and split up in a manner that none could catch up without running. From the front, which was already around the corner, no one could tell what had happened. It was not wise to charge up the train on a running horse, therefore I warned each driver that I was coming through fast. Naturally they wanted to know what was going on and I couldn't stop to say. Having been in the driver's seat, I knew how they felt, but then was not the time to stop and chat. Racing up to the wagon master, I called out to him to stop the train because there had been a bad accident and the wagons were split up over hundreds of yards. Two-way radios were needed in cases like this, but we could never get any help with them until the very end of the journey. This was always a sore spot with me, as I saw too many wrecks that needed help a lot faster than when it finally arrived. But then the original settlers didn't have them either. Garry halted the train and galloped back to check the damage.

Everyone was put back in line except the boys' ranch. Their horses were not hurt, God only knows why, and Walt had also escaped injury but did not find his glasses. The McCrossons wired that broken tongue and caught us at the water stop. If only all of the negative people that thought we would never reach the stockyards could have seen the determination of the McCrosson Boys' Ranch.

Chapter Thirty-seven

Just outside of the coliseum in San Antonio, we stopped for our last water stop of the day. The color guard went forward and seventeen of us picked up the colors and rode at the front of the wagon train most proudly. Bobby had driven up and walked up the line of wagons during the break. I ran toward him and knocked both our hats off. M. C. Hendry picked them up and waited for us to finish our greeting. Not everyone knew Bobby, so M. C. laughed when he said, "I assume this is your husband. No one else gets that much attention from you." We both laughed assuring him he was right. Jack and Joanna Bewly had come with Bobby to enjoy the festivities.

Carrying the Texas flag, I fell in beside Kay Lightfoot, who held the American flag at the front of the column directly behind the U.S. Cavalry from Fort Hood. We came into San Antonio in the grandest style any wagon train ever had in the history of the state. The woman that had accused me of taking her gear told me I had no right to carry the Texas flag as I was not born a Texan. I let her know right quick that it was a good thing Colonel Travis didn't feel the same way when one hundred eighty-two of the one hundred eighty-nine that fought with him at the Alamo were volunteers.

As the wagons came into the campgrounds and circled, our flag corp was stationed off to their right. Every teamster that passed saluted and cheered. They were glad to see their colors unfurrowed in the wind and that we had done something with the flags to honor the participants.

The second morning in San Antonio, O. C. Horn left the wagon train. It was sad to see him go as he had been there every step of the way. But home problems required his attention immediately. This was a sad part of the journey but it happened from time to time. Both he and his wife Kathryn would return at a later time and remain until the end.

Bobby and I, along with Jack and Joanna, drove downtown to take the river walk and see the Alamo up close. Since my move to Texas, I had always wanted to see the historical sight. My husband had said we would go some time but the time never presented itself. I kidded him then about how I finally got my wish to see San Antonio and the Alamo, but I didn't know I had to ride my horse to get there.

We lunched on the river and crossed the street to the shrine of the Alamo.

I was struck by the memorial as soon as I walked through the door. During the attack of the Alamo, volunteers from Gonzales sent all of the reinforcements they had. To this day, those reinforcements are represented during the thirteen days of observation on the anniversary of the battle. It was very emotional inside the building, especially the flag room. I had a lump in my throat that was not going down. There before me hung the flags of the volunteers of a century and a half ago. It represented a small band of men that gave up their lives to show this country what sacrifice really meant and what our freedom cost. It all happened right there where I stood.

Men are asked to remove their hats and there is absolutely no picture-taking or loud noise inside. For those that do not understand these rules, I cannot explain any further. The names of the original men that died at the Alamo are inscribed on plaques on the walls. The name Lightfoot is there. He was Kay Lightfoot's great granddaddy-in-law. The old reached and touched us once again.

Making a pilgrimage as we were doing had its moments of glory and its moments of attention, but standing there in the Alamo where the beginnings of this mighty state was founded had an impact that this wagoneer will never be able to put into words strong enough to tell.

March 2, 1986 the Texas Wagon Train rolled out of camp to circle the Alamo. We could not help but to think of the men of the Alamo. Our determination, and drive, and enthusiasm were at a high. The flag corp had been asked to ride at the rear of the train because San Antonio had a mounted palomino flag corp that was to lead the train around the Alamo. We would have liked to have had that distinct honor, however they had it and joined us four blocks from the Alamo and withdrew three blocks afterwards. We carried our flags seven miles at the rear.

To see the historical Alamo from the back of a horse carrying a Texas flag and knowing I had arrived on a wagon train can cause a tear. Add the fact that it was during the time of the siege, the thirteen days of glory, on an early Sunday morning, and it will move the toughest Texan to thank God and appreciate any rights he may have from that day forward. I can tell you, it can also cause a volunteer to be damn proud. It was a combination of honor, heartfelt emotion, and accomplishing a lifelong dream all locked into one. The men of the Alamo did not have a way out. We rode away with their memories in our hearts infinitely.

At our first water stop, Garry France told us we would

be crossing the first one thousand-mile mark in four more miles. Bobby was following our progress so I told him to post himself along the way and get some photos of the milestone. He had missed the Alamo circling because we came around the area about an hour earlier than what was announced on the radio. Our pace car driver, Sherry Anderst from Madison, South Dakota, would let us know when the exact moment came. We kept going, thinking it was just another step. After a while, Bobby would be waiting on each street block. I just kept telling him, "No. Not yet." Then he'd skipped a block. Of course, that block was the one. On a rise near a church in the middle of an intersection marked the spot. Lynndale and Broadway were the street names, just before the crest on a hill out of sight from my husband and his waiting camera. Jan France handed me a sign that was quickly written up showing 1000 with an arrow pointing down. I sat on Lady to meet every wagon as it passed, shaking hands and hollering like a group of wild people. It was an accomplishment that only those of us that had taken this outfit down the road could feel. The bystanders were treated to quite a display of affection and laughter. I held that sign until the last of the two "blue rooms" went by. Cecil Dobkins and John Gilbert had been with us all the way also. They saluted and were proud, too. We threw hats in the air and hugged and kissed—no easy task from the back of a horse. Later that evening I walked out onto a big lawn at the campsite and wrote a poem about the day:

> We've crossed the river of time,
> Shared bread and water together,
> Rode into valleys of history,
> Been blessed with God's good weather,

Set a horseback, driven teams,
Counted stars from beneath the trees,
Laughed and cried with heartfelt pride,
No boundaries do we see.

We've looked death in the face
And suffered some losses,
Heard Bells from the missions,
Knelt down before crosses.

Came through San Antonio,
Sitting tall in our saddles,
Following wagons,
That sing when they rattle.

Reached the first thousand miles
And hollered so they'd know
That the wagon train would always
Remember the Alamo!

Chapter Thirty-eight

The train stayed in San Antonio one more night before continuing on out of a town we had been in for so long we were beginning to wonder if we could get through it. Traveling four miles an hour, we would often think this about the bigger cities.

Bobby left that last night, and I cried marking the first time since I had started the journey I had done this, but that time it was hard and I wanted him to stay longer. We were going on out toward the western part of the state and wouldn't be back for a long time. After he drove away, I had a very serious attack of the melancholies again.

Our departure out of town was uneventful. Mark Morton and I were asked to set the pace for the train. Lady and I, Mark and Frances, his mule, rode out at the point, leading the wagon train. I can't speak for Mark but it was one of the highlights of the journey for me. We just rode along in silence listening to the musical tunes being sung in the lead wagon. Then Woody started to play the french harp as only Woody could do. Old tunes from a long time ago echoed out into the air to be picked up by a listener that was lucky enough to be within earshot.

Chapter Thirty-nine

The flu bug had finally caught up with the wagon master. Garry would not give into the malady; he was a man that had made a self-commitment to ride a horse every step of the way and would not give in at any cost. He could not talk and could barely hold his head up, yet he kept riding. He took medicine to help but the temperture changed so often from day to day and location to location that it was hard to heal under those conditions.

Garry had to turn back at some point on the trail to help the McCrosson outfit with a problem. When the wagons were ready to roll again, he had not made it back up to the lead yet. Jan asked me to give the "wagons ho!" I watched Garry do it often enough. Throwing back my head and standing up in my stirrups, I called them on and it wasn't half bad. Later, one of the drivers asked me if that was me calling or if Garry had hurt himself on the saddle horn. The humor of that group never died.

Just outside of Spring Branch, the rains came. Yellow slickers by the hundreds were put on, and we just kept on rolling. The campgrounds had been hit the hardest.

Milton Knebbe's Ranch was hosting us for the night, but mother nature had turned it into a horrible mud hole. The support vehicles that made it into camp before the storm were to stay in the pastures, but most of the others were directed to park outside of the grounds. Naturally, the wagon train was circled on the ranch, but all other vehicles were scattered out over a five mile radius. Many could not make it into camp to see the entertainment or enjoy slopping around in the mud, ankle deep, to watch our talent show that night. Hospitality was great; the mud was horrible. Mr. Oliver was out in the roadway directing traffic and trying to keep some type of order with over one hundred vehicles that had no place to go. Quinton McGown, always hosted our talent shows, but this night, the flu bug had gotten to him. He sent word to ask me if I could take over for him. With the help from my fellow wagoneers, we all helped make the evening enjoyable for our audience standing in the mud.

We left the Knibble Ranch to start our thirty-mile day. The previous day's rain was not through with us yet. To get to the ranch from the main roadway, a deep paved drainage area had to be passed over. The teams struggled with the slick surface. Saddle horses pulled some of the wagons. The train was very late getting out of the camp and on its way. Garry had to go back to the ditch area to help, leaving Vickie Hazzard, Jan France, and me to keep the wagons moving slowly to wait for the rest to catch up. Vickie posted herself on the curve and signaled to me to tell Jan that more wagons had made the crossing and that we needed to move up a ways to get them into line. Jan would then signal back, I called "wagons ho!" and we moved out. After about forty minutes of this, everyone was finally in line. Precious time had been lost but it could not be avoided. We would have yet another long day on the road, arriving late in camp.

We were seven miles outside of Blanco, Texas next to a sign tht said "Twin Sister." I had gone back down the train from the front to get the flag corp together to lead us into Blanco. The community was putting together a welcoming party for us in town around the city square. I had ridden back down the train talking to each flag carrier. My last volunteer nodded his head. I signaled my mare to turn, her right hind leg slipped into a hole, and quickly I gave her a free rein to jump clear. Her left leg slipped too; I can remember her falling back into the hole and thinking she was going to scramble out. The thought of jumping clear did not occur to me. Lady and I have been together ten years and she had never been off her feet with me. Clinging to her tightly with my legs, I was sure she would bring us out of danger. Oddly, I never saw the hole until we were in it. She was fighting so hard to gain her footing. Suddenly, she made one powerful lunge. We slipped for the third time, so I jumped and threw myself at the same time since I knew we were not going to make it. I covered my head with my arms in case she came over on top of me. I remember hearing a loud crack and it hit me—she had broken her leg. I jumped up to get out of the way and get Lady but I could not get my right leg to do anything. She then fell on top of me. Neither one of us could get away from the damn hole. I tried to crawl. My mind did not focus on me being hurt—only my horse. With every ounce of strength, I grabbed dirt, rocks, and whatever I could get up out of the hole. Then it hit me hard. Fire shot through my leg. I fell and could not move. I went down face first in the dirt and the leg would not do anything. The pain was so bad my breathing wouldn't even work. I tried to get up, calling for the mare. The accident happened near the back of the wagon train, and where so many people came from so fast, I will never know. Jo Ann Theilman was there to cradle my head and wipe the dirt out of my mouth and eyes. Jeff Sheppard came on the run and picked up one of my hands to soothe me and assure me help was on its way. Jo got a pillow from somewhere and put it under my head. No one knew what my injuries were so they couldn't turn me over. A policeman came and said an ambulance was on its way. I was a big help; I would not do anything until I saw Lady. I was probably a bit ugly about it, but I demanded to see her. She was led over to where I could see for myself if she had any injuries. The mare was fine. I will always remember Dr. Ken getting down on his hands and knees and promising me that Lady would be taken care of until I was back in the saddle again. A promise he never broke.

I'll also remember everyone helping me with tender words and feelings. Dr. Ken kept his word to me; my mare never missed a day of traveling with the wagon train, he also kept her in pretty good shape by having his two sons saddle her up and get out from time to time while I was healing.

I did not fare as well as Lady from the accident. An ambulance came and took me to the hospital in San Antonio. The diagnosis of a positive broken femur bone went with me. The pain was unbearable. My leg had been stretched out and bound to a board. Nelda was with me in the ambulance trying to keep my mind off the discomfort. Her husband, Jack French, followed in his car. My jokes were a little weak but I was going to be tough. When I had been loaded onto the gurney and taken away from the train, I smiled at Dr. Ken and sent him to tell everyone I was just fine, praying it would be true. The care I received was sloppy and nondiagnostic. The doctor told me after the second X-ray that nothing was broken and I was to see a doctor four or five days down the road if I felt it was necessary. A nurse gave me a shot that all but knocked me out. I will say the pain stopped, so did the feelings in my hands, feet, and tongue. I quite simply slipped into the twilight zone. Jack and Nelda literally put me back in the car in my fashionable wardrobe of a hospital gown and bedsheet. My Wranglers had been cut to ribbons, my boots cut and destroyed, and my shirt was lost somewhere along the line. Jack took me back to camp and the nurse's quarters. I can vaguely remember voices of concerned friends stopping by the trailer in the evening hours to see how I was. I was not aware of anything too clearly until the next morning when J. R. Newton came by to tell me he was moving the trailer up to the next camp and just to lie still. No problem—I could not move! That morning, I missed "wagons ho!" for the first time since we had pulled out of Sulphur Springs. I hated it. We were to camp on the L.B.J. Park grounds. I thought if I moved around I would feel better. First of all, I had to get my clothes, then assess the damage. A little groggy still, I made the supreme effort to get up. The leg would not move—period. It was time to call Bobby and get his help. I had told everyone not to call Bobby as I wanted him to hear my voice instead of a stranger's. This would keep him from worrying too much, I hoped.

My husband was not to be reached at that time. Returning to camp, I noticed a police car had pulled in bringing bad news to Mo and Vera Berg. His mother had passed away and they were to return to Forth Worth immediately. Mo said he would be glad to take me back with him. Ron Goff, one of the staff members of the train, had been moving me from vehicle to trailer then back to vehicle again. He helped me into the Berg truck and off we went.

We had stopped to call home. I sent a message through my landlady to get Bobby to meet me at the Berg residence. I do not know what my husband must have thought when he first saw me. Still in the hospital gown with the bedsheet around me, and sitting in a wheelchair, I must have been a sight. The next morning I went to a specialist for the injury. Everyone was so worried about me. I wasn't. After all, I was still alive. Dr. Wilson told me that I had shredded the entire muscle that connects to the femur bone and attaches to the hip. It was turned into a mass much like a bloodclot. He advised me to take therapy and consider surgery plus resting at home for six weeks while the leg healed properly. I said I could not do this. I had a wagon train to catch and would be back on it in two days. He uttered words about me not being a normal person. I in turn told him he was absolutely correct, but I was not going to stay home. He asked why. I tried to put into words how one feels about roots, self-dedication, and a wagon train in the year 1986, also how this would heal better if I went and spent time back where I felt I had to be. This is not an easy thing to convince a specialist of medicine in this day and age. It was understandable. He tried to see it my way, gave me medication, and sent me off with a promise that I would return as soon as possible.

My journey back to Forth Worth also gave me the opportunity to visit with my daughter, Donya, who would make me a grandmother before the end of the trail. Her arrangements were to have the child at my home with a midwife. I would miss being there when she needed another woman's helping hand. Not to mention just having mother around. However, the wagon train was calling to me and no matter how I felt about anything else, I had to get back. The thought of not returning never occurred to me. There would be a slight handicap for a while, but my crutches would still allow me to go just about anywhere.

Bobby had me back at the wagon train area after only two days in Forth Worth. The campsite had been changed

three times, and we could not find it. So we posted ourselves on a street corner in downtown Kerrville. I had not
taken the time to see the wagon train pass by in its entirety.
It was a beautiful sight, from the lead wagon driven by
Jan France to the very end. Starting with Jan, she held
onto the lines to the mules and hollered jumping up and
down on the seat at the least ten inches. No one had known
I was going to return that day or even if I could return. I
would yell out my greeting to them. My wagon train family
was just as happy to see me as I was to see them. It had
only been three days but felt like a month. I believe my
husband wasn't as apprehensive about leaving me with all
the strangers as he had been at first. All the way to the
last wagon the welcomes were the same. When the train
stopped for lunch, I approached Albert Nicely to see if I
could ride in his wagon. He had made the back of his
wagon comfortable for his wife Alice, as she broke her foot
the first day out of Sulphur Springs. The day before my
accident she had the cast taken off and was riding again.
It was my turn to ride in the unofficial recuperation wagon.
Albert kindly welcomed me to his vehicle. As it turned
out, I rode many a mile in this wagon during my convales-
cence.

Mr. and Mrs. Walker from Sulphur, Oklahoma, had
become very good friends of mine. We had gotten together
many times over the miles. Mrs. Walker walked across the
circle of wagons to meet me as we came into camp and
stopped for the night. We met in the center of the circle.
Though a very small woman, she sure gave me a huge
bear hug. We stood and visited as Bobby brought the car
around to meet me. Mrs. Walker was a favorite amongst
all of us. Both of the Walkers were heart patients, but took
care of all their own work, carrying water, harnessing, and
the rest of the labor along the trail. In their retirement

years, they had joined the train to travel with us to Eden, Texas. Relatives were to meet them there, then, they'd go back to Oklahoma and home. Bobby drove up. We left the Walkers and others that had joined in to welcome me back to the train. I wanted to see my mare. Lady looked real good, but I could tell she missed the constant handling I had given her when we were traveling closely. We had our camp by the beautiful Guadalupe River; Bobby led Lady down to the bank to drink. Returning to the circle, we saw an ambulance coming into the camp grounds. I followed it with my eyes, wondering who was in trouble now. The ambulance pulled up in front of the Walker's wagon. I had Bobby hurry over to the back of their wagon, jumping out of the car as fast as I could. My special friend, Helen Walker, was lying on the ground. My heart was broken for her. She had somehow slipped out of the wagon that she had climbed in and out of at least two hundred times, and lost her footing. Her leg was broken near the hip joint. I leaned over her and wiped my tears. I would miss this caring lady for she had been a sparkle in my days. There was no way she could make it back to the train; Eden was five days away. Mrs. Walker had surgery the next morning, and remained in the hospital for about ten days. Mr. Walker, being a real trouper, continued on to Eden. Someone drove him back to see his wife daily. When he left us in Eden, I could not bring myself to go up to him. Saying good-bye was not in my voice box for this wonderful man. I watched him work with his animals from a distance and said my parting words to him only in my mind. We would meet again.

I slept restlessly that night; my leg throbbed so hard I couldn't believe it. But I knew I best face the fact this was going to be a way of life for a while. I would just keep my pain pills at hand.

We traveled up the Gaudalupe River after leaving Kerrville. The river was magnificent. Those bridges we crossed were mostly made of cement over big drain culverts about ten inches above the water. The scenery was outstanding: hills, water, trees, and covered wagons—what a sight! As I looked back down the road after making a turn, I could see back through the trees and watched the wagons cross one of the bridges. The sun's reflection on the river made it look like silver. A bright reflection and the wagons rolling over the bridges with no railing looked as if wagons and teams were moving across the surface of the water. Some of the wonders of nature can create a breathtaking effect.

Chapter Forty

Mr. Felix Kline was eighty-six years old. He had waited for the Texas Wagon Train to get to his ranch for a very long time. Though he was not in the best of health, his spirit was as strong as ever. He sat in his car right where the wagons were circled, watching with amazement each one of us come in. This was the day he had waited for. Mr. Kline was on an oxygen machine to aid his breathing. Jan had jumped down from the lead wagon to go to him and thank him for being there to greet us. He looked straight into her eyes and said, "I made it. I lived long enough to see the Texas Wagon Train on my land." Tears were streaming down Mr. Kline's face. Jan could not hold back hers either. How can you hide an emotion such as that welcome, unmatched anywhere, from such a dignified country gentleman? The pioneers had ridden out of the past to touch the empire he had prepared. We thank you, Mr. Kline, for reaching out and touching us.

On the Kline Ranch, we were greeted by a good sized stock pond. The young people of the train, especially, took the horses and waded out into the water to cool them off and just relax. It would be close to try to guess who had the most fun, the horses or the kids. Boys and girls alike would jump from the backs of the animals. A lot of the horses just lay down in the water and stuck their heads up to breath. It must have felt real good as most of them did it. Lawn chairs were spread out all under the trees along the banks as many of us just watched the youngsters perform. The weather was very warm, unlike just a few days previous when it was downright cold.

After the sun set outside, visitors came into camp from the outlying areas and joined with some of the wagoneers to play tunes on guitars and sing old country songs. The music drifted out across camp and touched everyone's ears, I'm sure. One of our memory-making evenings.

Chapter Forty-one

After leaving the Kline Ranch, we crossed the Guadalupe River again and rode along canyon walls that nature had prepared with such art. The famous YO Ranch was our next destination. Many of the ranch hands were at the beautiful entrance to verbally welcome each and every one of us. There were lots of windmills as far as we could see. In fact, the YO is serviced by twenty-four all together. They are the ranch's only water supply. When Captain Charles Schriener came to the area in the 1840s at the age of fourteen, he started a legend that still lives today.

Many exotic animals live on the YO. We were to be privileged to see a good number of them before the end of our stay.

The original settlers of last century came to mind in strength the next morning as we crossed the hills of the YO Ranch, passing over dry creekbeds close to exotic animals, the famous hunting areas, winning quarter horses, legendary longhorns, and acres and acres of rocks. Now we knew how or forefathers traveled to find and settle new lands, as we crossed just a portion of that fifty thousand acres of working ranch. We traveled on rocks. Everywhere we looked there was nothing but rocky grounds as far as the eye could see. The best way for me to describe this ride is to tell someone to go out onto their driveway and place eight to twelve inch rocks closely together, then get a bicycle and remove the rubber tires. Mount that bicycle and ride across those rocks on the steel rims. You will have a slight idea of what we wagoneers went through.I rode in the stagecoach that Rudi Nelson drove. The stagecoach was sponsored by Triland Corporation of Dallas, Texas. I bounced around in the stage like a rubber ball. My leg throbbed yet I still couldn't think of any other place I would rather be. Now the world knows I, along with my traveling companions, had totally lost all sense of realism.

To have the privilege of crossing this ranch in a stagecoach, and looking out the windows to see the exotic animals as we passed by knowing an entire wagon train was following, is a special memory.

At the bottom of a long steep descent ending near the merging of the Llano Rivers and Kimble County lies Junction, Texas. As the covered wagons rolled down the hill toward camp, they were treated to a magnificent sight of a Texas flag atop the high cliffs, waving in greeting to welcome our pioneers. Nelda French and I had ridden in the stagecoach that day when Jeff Sheppard came riding up to tell me that the state troopers wanted to talk to me.

The first thing I thought of was what tragedy had happened at home. I became so worried it was almost unbearable. Nelda tried to talk about everything she could think of to get my mind off of my worry. Bless her heart, she spoke of everything from the trees outside the windows to just anything that came to mind. We rode along like that for over an hour, and I was plenty worried by the time we stopped again. My handicap with my leg did not help; I would have jumped out of the stagecoach and chased the patrol car down if I could have to eliminate my worry. As the stage stopped, I watched a patrol car pull up alongside us. A giant of a man stepped out and came toward me. Delbert Roberts, the trooper, approached the stage that sits up off the ground so high, it took two very big men to get me up there. He extended his hand in greeting quickly adding that I was to be the first captive off the wagon train. I must have looked rather dumb, for he added that I was invited to join the staff of the school and go before the students of the sixth, seventh, and eight grades to tell them the story of the wagon train before the wagoneers reached the city limits, giving them an idea of what to expect. I believed it to be a great idea and accepted. He picked me up out of the stage like I was nothing, and put me in the patrol car. I did not have time to tell anyone where I was going. What my traveling companions must have thought of me at the time, I have no idea. Nelda told them later, I'm sure, but all they saw was me being whisked away in a police car without a word. Trooper Roberts took me to lunch first. I noticed most of the people looked at us rather strangely. I was dressed in my usual wagon train clothing, walking with the aid of my crutches, could have stood a bath, and looked a little shabby. Now why should anyone think anything of me sitting at a table, eating lunch with a state trooper? Don't prisoners in transport resemble this all the time?

From lunch, we drove to the school and were met by Delbert's wife, Opal, and his sister-in-law, Tommie Gaston. The principal, Mr. Templeton, made an official welcome.

Opal Roberts had been responsible for the idea of having a wagoneer come to the school and speak to the students. An English teacher, she knew the importance of the journey to the young people. After introductions were made, we all met in the auditorium, where the students had been called for an impromptu meeting. Mr. Templeton made the introductions, and I walked out onto the stage in my less than perfect appearance. The only good thing I can really say about my clothing was that I definitely looked like a traveler. The students were excellent. I told them about our journey and everything I could think of. Then I asked them to feel free to ask whatever questions they wanted. They had been breathlessly still as I told them about the passing of Pam Burchell, plus roared with laughter at my answer to when to do the laundry. I simply told the truth. You can find your cleanest dirty shirt twice and wear your wranglers at least seven days on the road. However, when you are down to the last pair of clean underwear, it's time to do the laundry. Their attention was all the thanks I needed. Young people of today deserve more credit than they are given. Mr. Templeton had given me thirty minutes to present my story. Fifty minutes later I asked him how much time I had left and he said there was almost ten minutes to go. I will always remember those students. Later on in the evening, most of them came out to the campsite and walked among us, having an insight they were wide-eyed and felt most comfortable with all of their questions.

Mr. Templeton returned me to camp after my meeting with the students. The wagons were just rolling into camp down off of the steep roadway into town. I told the principal a little bit about each wagoneer and wagon as they passed by us to circle in camp. A Texas flag was waving its greeting to all from high atop the cliff as the wagons paraded by. Opal and Tommie had made arrangements to pick me up later for a shower. I wouldn't turn that invitation down. None of us would!

Junction, Texas had been visited by another Texas history writer, James Michener, while he was researching for his recent novel *Texas*. Most of the readers on the wagon train could be seen at one time or another reading this novel. I was one of them. Now I was doing my own research to chronicle this piece of Texas history.

I was to guest with Tommie Ann that night. She lives in the old Las Lomas Hotel, a very fine old stately building that dates back to the beginnings of the town. It was built on the bend of the river where the North and South Llano Rivers meet.

The entertainment provided for the wagoneers came from the youth of Junction. They had worked very hard to put together a program of square dancing. It was very well done and appreciated by all of us.

I watched them closely. Some were from the assembly I had taken part in earlier that day. Their sharing time for the wagon train was wonderful. I watched one young man in particular, Rendon Roberts—he was Opal's son. As I leaned against my crutches, the students passed by to talk to me more about the train. Quentin McGown caught all of our attention at 7:25, when everyone was asked to please look toward the cliffs at the entrance of the campgrounds where we had come down the hill. Flood lights had been set up and at precisely 7:30 all of the lights of the park would be cut and the cliffs would come to life. For the first time ever, flood lights were going to light the sheer rocks. We all turned toward the cliff. The lights were cut all around camp. We stood in the darkness only seconds; then a gasp could be heard everywhere. The cliffs came to life. The Texas flag was still on top of the highest point glowing with warmth. Everyone started to sing "The Eyes of Texas Are Upon You."

Music floated out across the night air. Most of us stood frozen just to see the awesome sight. The tears flowed and the wagoneers will always remember that most honored moment Junction put before us.

The next morning just before the wagons rolled out of camp to parade through town and pass by the school as we were always so conscientious of doing, we heard a report that students would not be allowed out of the classrooms just to watch the wagon train pass by. This notice had come to them from a state level. Therefore, when the train passed the school, a fire drill was being held and all the students just happened to be on the street corner when we passed. I noticed the students at the end of the line of young peole as we rolled by. Most of them had been in the auditorium the previous day. I was riding in Albert Nicely's wagon, and, after making the turn away from the school, I looked over my shoulder to wave a final farewell to those wonderful youngsters. Up to that point, I had not broken down and cried openly on the trip, but their smiling, caring faces triggered that emotion and the tears came streaking down my face. Their enthusiam was going to be hard to match anywhere. Thank you, Junction.

Chapter Forty-two

The next camp, on a private ranch, was a reminder of the YO—nothing but rocks almost everywhere. I walked up the hill to see Lady as I did every day, and took an apple. She would see me coming and start calling to me. We usually stood and discussed the day's events. I don't know if she got as much out of it as I did, but I know she always looked forward to me coming. It was probably the apple.

As we traveled further down the road, everyone was good friends in no time. After all, when you are sharing such close quarters, it's hard not to get to know one another. I felt a little uncomfortable about this blue room stuff in the beginning, but the further we got down the road one had to shed one's shyness about some things and the blue room was right there at the top of the list. It got to where a gentleman would walk out of a unit and face a line of pioneers waiting, and not give a second thought about holding the door for a lady even if it was the door to the outhouse. There is humor in this chivalry, but one had to have been there to really appreciate it. On March 14th we had stopped for lunch break. Mike Lowery was telling Perry Jo Frost stories about the Martians landing. Another wagoneer walked amongst us passing out food to those that had none that day. Others lay on the ground in various areas napping. The horses and mules shifted their hind legs, then found a comfortable stance to nap themselves. Just by walking along the line of wagons, one could find a gathering of strangers that had become lifetime friends within a short time. We were all together doing the civilized mock-up of times gone by. We were all normal everyday citizens of Texas and America—or were we?

Chapter Forty-three

While recuperating from my accident, I took the opportunity to travel in several different wagons to get better acquainted with the teamsters of the various wagons. Albert Nicely was the first one I rode with; plus his was the wagon

I traveled in the longest—mainly because I had learned how to get into and out of his wagon without bothering anyone to help me. Every traveler had enough things to do without aiding a handicap. At the same time, there was usually always someone that offered to help in any way they could. I was just stubborn and wanted to do it myself. On the different occasions when I hurt myself badly because of this self-aid attitude, I still question my reasoning.

I started to ride in different wagons and change my personal scenery now and again. How some of those teamsters didn't get stir crazy, I will never know. Debbie Johnson, Albert Nicely, Doug Kafka, Fred Shivers, James Simmons, Miss Hazel, J. W. Jines, and many many more had to stay in the same place behind the wagon in front of them and not see anything else directly in front of them for over three thousand miles. They made that choice the same as I did—riding a horse. So maybe they thought I was uncomfortable also. As we entered Eden, Texas, I had hopped a ride with Jim Saylor in his Conastoga Wagon. Jim hails from the state of Maryland, and represented the state very well. He always wore a uniform every day and looked the part of the trains that rolled a century ago. Jim and Patrick Anderson boosted me into the seat of the Conastoga at noon, and there I stayed. That particular wagon sat up very high. The viewpoint was great and the ride was smoother than I had expected.

The wagon train came into Eden, a small town, but the entire population came out to welcome the train. People lined the streets, sat on top of the buildings, and stood ten deep on the sidewalks. It was heartwarming to see such a sight. We were tired and weary but those faces and smiles, coupled with the enthusiam anyone could offer as a welcome made the pioneers of the eighties come alive with excitement themselves. No matter what, we always found the extra energy to greet our fans with dignity and fervor. The electricity between the welcomers and the wagoneers is what truly kept the Texas Wagon Train going down the road. How could we ever deny those people the right to take just one moment of their lives to appreciate themselves? Actually, that's what we did. In so many ways people came to pay homage to a life gone by, a life that brought them to where they stood in modern-day times. These welcomers could see why they needed to keep going into a world that may seem rather bleak sometimes, going on to when it would get better with harder work and self-belief. We were living proof of that. The past reached the present again. My brother and sister-in-law, Kenneth and Bobbie Stepp, were waiting for me when the wagons rolled into Eden. It was great to see a face from the family. The wagoneers were a close family, but to see someone from home meant we could share a real member of our families with our adopted family. It was done by everyone all along the entire journey. We loved sharing our life on the trail with folks from home. Kenneth and Bobbie took me to dinner after I made them walk all over camp so I could introduce them to everyone I could find. They also drove me to Balinger for the night after they helped me take care of my camp chores. This ended up being a very special week for me. I was treated to two showers and sleeping in a real bed twice. Kenneth and Bobbie had a wonderful room. They had been in the area for over a week on business plus added two days to stay and meet the wagon train. When the day's journey overcame me and it was time to turn in, they said they would sleep on the floor. I was too tired to argue, but it just did not seem right that they should give up their bed to sleep on the floor while I took up all of that huge king sized bed. The room was carpeted and it looked wonderful to me compared to some of the surfaces I had tried to sleep on. My leg was throbbing so bad I didn't want to make a big deal of the situation. However, the arrangement wasn't right until I realized they were doing exactly what they wanted to do.

Upon returning to the camp early the next morning, I couldn't help but rub in the fact that I had had my second hot shower so far that week. My dear friends turned their backs on me and walked away. I laughed and they kept walking.

Right out of camp in Eden, on our way to Eola, we passed a retirement home. As usual, all of the residents that were able sat waiting for the wagons to pass. We always hollered extra for them, and this was no exception. Two resident ladies were sitting so very close together in their wheelchairs. The woman in front had her head held high, listening to every sound she could. It was clear her vision was gone. Very close to her was what appeared to be a longtime close friend. The friend was leaning ever so close to the blind lady's ear and telling her everything she could see with her own vision. The blind woman had a look of total amazement on her dear face. She would raise her hand toward us and we knew she would always remember the wagon train. We waved back and she became more excited. A person who could see well could not have shared this moment with us any more deeply than she did. God love her. I was busy trying to clear the tears from my eyes from being witness to this wonder of sights when I looked into the very last window of the nursing home. I do not know why I cast my eyes in that direction, but from behind the last window of the home, sitting in another wheelchair, was the solomn face of another aged resident. One that could very easily have come from last century. I turned fully toward this lonely-looking patient and waved to her. She all but jumped out of her confinement to return my recognition. Both of her arms went toward the ceiling.

She moved in her chair as I am sure she had never done before. You could see the strength to point toward a pioneer waving only to her. She had been spotted and would always know that the wagon train saw her from behind her walls of confinement. I would not be able to leave Eden, Texas with dry eyes. I'm sure I was not alone.

Eola, Texas is located south of San Angelo and has a population of two hundred. When the wagon train rolled into town, there were four to five thousand welcomers there to greet us. We were camped all over town with our usual circle of wagons right in the center of all the activities.

When the teams were unhitched, they were each guided by skilled hands out through the crowds with the utmost care. Most of the onlookers moved to allow the animals to pass, but were still close enough to touch them. It is difficult to picture such a small community having so many people come out just to see us, but it happened.

Chapter Forty-four

Our seventy-seventh day on the road found us looking to enter the city of San Angelo. We had not had a very good reception in all of the larger towns we rolled through; therefore, we were a little leary of this town also. Just as the day began for us, the cars were lined up alongside the highway all the way into the city. There was twenty-five miles of cars; it was hard to believe all the people there to greet us but the line never ended or stopped or had a break anywhere along our route. The most surprising part of this day of travel was the wind; it blew again today and we could not escape its biting attention. Dust cut through just about anything we had on. One of the photographers, taking some shots of the day, had a lens chipped because of the force of the dusty wind. While riding a horse in this type of weather, it is easier for a rider to turn a collar up and a hat down. A teamster must hold the lines to the teams and keep his or her head up to watch the road, therefore their faces are turned to the wind. The true soul of this wagon train showed through on those days. It was cold and not a fit day to travel with the high winds whipping the dirt everywhere. But the pioneers always kept rolling forward to the next camp—the next town.

San Angelo greeted the wagon train with the same enthusiasm as the little tiny town of Eola. This was the first time I could compare the hospitality of a small community to that of a larger town. San Angelo hosted us with warmth and pride that was obvious to all. I can say they literally thought of everything, including filling the propane bottles for those that had them—at no cost. The people had open hearts and very caring minds. We were all ready for our layover day; the wagons had traveled sixteen days in a row without a rest day. Our laundry was backed up and supplies were short. We had wonderful shower facilities at the college. On a large chalk board in the locker room, we all wrote a message of gratitude, and we meant it.

The dinner provided for us was more than good; it was excellent. On our second day, buses were provided to take the wagoneers to Fort Concho to witness the honor guard and the formal flag ceremonies, displays of different artists at work, and to have another dinner with entertainment.

By the time we rolled out of camp, we were ready for the next camp. One thing about traveling in this manner, we always knew we had a next camp and another day to travel. Therefore, getting ready to roll was not a chore or a sad moment.

The Concho River provided a backdrop of magnificence when we passed by on our way out of camp—trees and green grass that stretched on forever. The pathway led us for quite a while under bridges and alongside nothing but beauty. Scenery such as this would not be a regular sight for a long while as we were entering into the roadways of west Texas towards El Paso. A lot of dry days were in store for the wagoneers. We rolled beneath bridges that stopped the train, as some of the flags had to be lowered to prevent broken poles. It was amusing to read the signs posted under the bridges: DO NOT STOP UNDER BRIDGES.

We were told to gather wood wherever we could find it alongside the roadway as our supply was out. We were also told to stock up on supplies for they would not be easily obtainable either. We would be close to the earlier pioneers in our travels, depending on our own abilities and self-help. A century may have passed by but the planning and survival was the same. We were meeting the elements of nature and ready to roll.

Chapter Forty-five

Early in the morning when camp comes to life, the animal sounds are accurate alarm clocks. After feeding time, the teams are harnessed and the saddle horses readied. I always loved to look around at my wagon train family and see who was present and accounted for, as some cannot ride every day for various reasons such as not having a remount, or perhaps not feeling well. Remounts are backup horses to replace others that need a bit more rest or are sick.

I rode in Albert Nicely's wagon, as usual. During the lunch break, Albert wanted to carry a few more children and wanted to know if we had enough room. I told him, "You bet," but I removed myself to make sure. This turned into a good idea. Albert told me not to leave until he saw where I was going. The McCrosson Boys' Ranch traveled directly in front of Albert's wagon and on that day, the boys were not in the back. After getting permission, I managed to hop in and rearrange the bed to suit my comforts whereupon I curled up and slept all the way to camp. It was like a luxury to my tired body. I can tell the truth now because my husband won't read this for months. My leg bothered me so bad I could not sleep at night and just could get around. But this stubborn determination of mine would not let me stop. I was aware that permanent damage could stem from this, but I could not give up. Sorry, dear.

I walked out amongst the camp one night to enjoy the company of each camp fire. Everyone offered such warm hospitality. Two or three families would group together, tell stories, or sing songs. They would simply share something. I will always think of those visits from time to time because of the warmth that came from not just the welcomed fires in the chill air, but the people themselves.

Chapter Forty-six

Bernhart, Texas greeted us with a marvelous welcome. People had ridden to the entrance of the camp on horseback and covered wagon. The time was turned back a century again; they all sat on their horses and waved greetings and welcomes. What a sight. This was one of the times along the route that the year just couldn't be 1986. A policeman in uniform was the only clue to modern-day times at that moment.

Much later that same evening, after the program from the citizens of the community were over, I knew I had overdone another day. Returning to my home, which was

Susan Whitfield's camper for now, I was no more than fifty paces from the door and could not take one more step. The pain shot up my leg and there was no movement. Through my tears, I saw a lit cigarette. In the darkness all cigarettes look the same, but the camper the glow was coming from looked like Ed Smith. I called out to him and he stepped toward me. I tried to explain what was going on. Ed knew me and needed no explanation. Picking me up, he took me to the camper and chewed me out in a fatherly, brotherly, friendly way, and I for once agreed with him. I had to be more careful.

Chapter Forty-seven

Big Lake, Texas spread a welcome mat for the wagoneers that many talked about for the rest of the journey. We were to stay two nights. The wind literally blew us into town. The townsfolk said the wind always blew.

Our nurse told me she had a new kind of wrap for my leg if I wanted to try it. I did and my leg felt great.

Big Lake's VFW was giving a dance for the wagoneers that evening, and I didn't feel like being alone. I rode over with five others. I couldn't dance but wanted to have a little fun. As I walked into the dance hall, I spotted a gentleman on crutches. Maneuvering my own sticks over to him, I asked for the next dance. Everybody thought it was funny but his wife. I've often wondered just what that woman thought I could do to him. The sad part was I really would have danced.

I found myself a very comfortable spot on the wall and leaned. Everyone passed by and greeted me and left their jackets for me to watch. Draping the jackets over my crutches just made it more comfortable for me, as the armrests became deeply padded. Leo Miller and Swede bought me a beer and the music was good. I read the sticker on the wall beside me that stated the capacity for the room was not to exceed one hundred twenty-five. No one needed a calculator to see we had exceeded that number. The certificate was from the fire marshall, whom I was sure must have caught the first stage out of town when we came in.

More wagoneers came drifting by my spot along the wall. We were all laughing and having a fun time. I had a pocket full of change to call Bobby. Surrounded as I was, I missed him a lot. I was talking to Nelda when all of a sudden, Bobby appeared right in front of me. I yelled and grabbed him tight, knocking our hats off, of course. It was swell to see him. Aunt Florence had driven in with him. Now I had my family to share with my friends again. Aunt Florence loved all of the stories I always shared with Bobby. Big Lake hosted the wagon train with hospitality and pride. It looked like every citizen in town came to entertain us, serve us a meal, dance, sing, or play games. It all went on throughout our stay. I missed most of this wonderful stop, as I lay down to rest Saturday afternoon and never got up until late Sunday evening. I did not know how exhausted I was until then. The clerk in the motel office very kindly took all of my laundry and washed it—again a wonderful extension of welcome from a stranger.

Chapter Forty-eight

On our way to Rankin and other points we noticed it was not unusual to see a rider or someone from a wagon jump suddenly to the ground and pick up a piece of wood alongside the road. The winds whipped the flags. In south

Texas we were very warm. Now heading northwest, we were back to the cold again. It was time again for chaps, gloves, heavy jackets, and extra long johns, or whatever it took to try to stay comfortable in the coldest of winds. During lunch, the wind was still blowing strong. We must have eaten one pound of dirt each before we moved out on the road again. At that point, it was probably best that we did not know this was the first pound of many. Also, the bar ditches were full of thorny bushes; caution had to be taken at every step. Through the strong winds and trying to keep our eyes covered, where the horses walked had to be watched carefully to avoid injury. The thorns could puncture a vehicle tire easily and would cripple a horse in an instant.

The winds spun the windmills we passed as if they had to catch every bit of energy possible. I looked out across the drylands of west Texas and saw a dust cloud being stirred by a small band of sheep. It was hard to imagine how these creatures could survive out there where nothing grew. Those sheep followed parallel with the train for a long time. Caution kept them at a distance. Nature and man watched one another with wonder.

When the first settlers came to west Texas, I could not imagine what made them stop and stay in the area. The local residents along our route would tell us of their great-great grandparents of the 1800s coming to this land, finding their homelands there in west Texas, and building from that point forward. My only thoughts were of how only the most hardy could even attempt it. Nothing appeared to grow except jackrabbits and rattlesnakes.

Chapter Forty-nine

Rankin, Texas, fed the wagon train a wonderful meal. We had traveled thirty miles and were ready for something delicious. With their homemade spaghetti, salads, cakes, and everything else, they were a wonderful welcoming sight to us. Their attitudes toward the wagoneers made up for that terrible wind. A personal milestone for me was reached in Rankin. I leaned my crutches against the wall and walked away. It was a slow pace and not without pain, but it was time to get on with walking unaided. I still had my brace and all of the support it gave. Everyone was concerned and I appreciated their feelings. A few setbacks made me conscientious of my progress. To travel in the capacity we were and not have full use of both sets of limbs was not easy. Therefore, I took each new step with care and knew I'd make it all the way. Getting Lady back was next. First I had to teach my leg to bend again.

Chapter Fifty

One of the spokespeople for the community of McCamey rode in the lead wagon as the wagons rolled into town. A statement they made was echoed throughout the state as we passed into and back out of their towns along our route. They always noticed things about their area in relation to the trees and plants and just the general appearance of their towns. Without fail, they would say, "I sure did not know my town looked like this." Traveling four miles an hour as we always did, one had time to see the surrounding area in a more absorbing manner.

At the lunch stop between McCamey and the open camp the night before our arrival into Fort Stockton, everyone had tended to their stock, eaten most of their lunches, and just stood around in general to visit as we always did on the trail. I passed everyone along the line of wagons speaking and exchanging quips of this and that on my way to the blue room. I was riding in Miss Hazel's wagon, driving while she rested that day. I walked back to the front of the train to get back in the wagon, when someone ask me if I had seen Nelda yet. She and I had just spoken to one another not five minutes earlier, so I said yes. Then Glyn Pearce made the comment that Nelda was lucky she wasn't killed instantly. I spun around and asked what he was talking about. My very special friend had just been kicked by the mule she was riding that day. She had reached into the saddlebags to get a snack. The plastic wrap on the food bothered the mule, and he swung around and kicked her in the side and the head. I hurried over to where Nelda was on the ground. It was always such a shock to see one of the wagoneers hurt and not up readying for the next move. I knelt down beside her; our medical staff of the train was with her and the police came quickly. They asked me if Nelda's husband Jack should be called. I knew how to reach him, and considering the head injury, I decided the quickest we could reach Jack, the better. An ambulance was on its way. Nelda was not fully conscious, she was not making clear conversation, and she was totally unaware of what had happened to her. A blanket was stretched over her, tent style, to keep the strong winds and dust off. I leaned over very closely to ask Nelda if she knew who I was. She tried to focus her eyes. I already had her hand in mine. Recognizing my voice, she asked me to stay with her as she was transported into Fort Stockton to the hospital. It was strange how our rolls were being reversed from when she had ridden with me to San Antonio.

I stayed with her until Jack drove in. The small hospital

was across the street from where we would have our camp in Fort Stockton. Nelda had broken four ribs and suffered a slight conclusion. When the mule turned to kick at the noise, he had knocked her sideways. This move saved her life; she was moving away from the animal when the blows came. When I returned to camp, I knew my friend would be going home and not back to camp; she was hurt too seriously to ride. I can remember my thoughts: *Damn.*

We had a layover day in Fort Stockton. Nelda had lots of us to visit her. She had come all the way and was a very popular figure around camp. Garry France went over to see her the previous night from camp to bid her well. Along with many, many wagoneers, Nelda had not realized we all cared so deeply. Fort Stockton did something for the wagoneers that would not be duplicated again. We were privileged to have a meal of all the fresh shrimp we could eat. Out in the dry lands, it was an unbelievable thought, let alone a reality. Everywhere one would look under the serving tent, you could see piles and piles of shrimp shells stacked on wagoneer's plates.

Sheriff Bruce and Martha Wilson walked amongst us and joined in to help us celebrate our stay in Fort Stockton. Martha took the time to meet me when I came into Fort Stockton with Nelda; she is a caring person and offered warmth and hospitality wherever we needed it.

We had reached the end of the line for a while, that is, as far as populated areas and towns to meet our needs for supplies and repairs go.

Fort Stockton was a pleasant relief in the desert. We rolled out of camp right by the hospital that Nelda was in. Word came to us that she had been rolled to where she could see us. Naturally, we left her with a loud get well wish. We knew she'd be back somewhere down the road.

Right outside of camp, Cody France came running up

alongside the train to get Garry. We did not know what happened, but they both turned and headed back toward camp. Martha Wilson came out to us later and brought news that Garry's daughter, Reka, had been thrown from her horse and injured seriously. Again we would wait anxiously for final word and pray for her. Martha let us know that Garry would not be able to ride; he was on his way to the Odessa hospital with Reka. This would be the very first day Garry would miss on the trail. Some of us even had the thought of him still riding into camp, but behind us a few hours. In the meantime, we had to keep going. Along our route that day, the usual crowds were there to greet us. One viewer, off a way from the rest, caught my eye because of his pet on a leash. The man had a coyote. It was a beautiful animal and very well-mannered. As the train passed by, the coyote became nervous and put his two front feet up on the man's leg. Reaching down, gentleness and calm came immediately. What a treat to see one of our night howlers up close. The trip was far from over and hundreds had called across the nights' air as we slept. The water stop brought more excitement. One of the wagons from the rear had a runaway just as we pulled up to the water tanks. Quick action from our riders once again saved injuries. The accidents had been so pre-valent, all of the wagoneers were trying hard to be more cautious.

Sheriff Bruce and Martha were near the entrance to our next camp, out of Fort Stockton. Sheriff Wilson had displayed professionalism and hospitality at its best throughout our stay in Pecos County.

Word passed quickly throughut camp: Reka was on her way back to camp. She was not as seriously hurt as had been previously believed. What a relief.

Chapter Fifty-one

Most of the young people on the wagon train probably left Sulphur Springs with visions of adventure and an easy trip on their minds. This, of course, was not the case at all. Hard work seven days a week was what happened. I saw youngsters of all ages toughen up, learn, and experience a new life they never knew existed. Some took longer, much to the chagrin of both parents and other wagoneers. On the whole, however, the young people of the wagon train walked into history, sharing time and experiences that will follow their steps and help all of them toward better lives.

Our wagon train school helped educate twenty-five students along the way. Each of the school days were filled with the necessary curriculum that is required. At the same time, the students, along with their teachers, participated in historic field trips all over the state. On top of tending to livestock, going down the road, and getting an education, our kids met a challenge that forced them to the limits. To me, they represented the youth of Texas and America with strength and intelligence. Their families must be very proud of them. Young people like this are our future leaders—the growing backbone of the nation. These students and many more we met along the route are a complement to the ancestors we represented as the wagons rolled.

Chapter Fifty-two

The day before we crossed the half way point of our journey, we celebrated Kevin Goff's birthday. Again we were quartered in an open camp, which was just a nice way of saying we were in a cow pasture. Doug Kafka, the wrangler wagon teamster, had made Kevin a pretty cake. Doug presented the cake to Kevin as a large group gathered around. Kevin took great care in trying to cut the pastry and serve it. Roars of laughter went up when all of his attempts failed and the "cake" was discovered to be a large quantity of cow manure! The next day was Easter. Camp always came to life between four-thirty and five A.M. On that particular day, we were to have our early Easter services. By flashlight, the stock was tended to and we gathered by a large bondfire in the center of the circle of wagons. Fred Shivers had made a crown of thorny vines and hung it on a cross by the blazing glow. The services began beneath a dark Texas sky, and about as close to our maker as we could possibly get. At the conclusion of our services, we all turned toward the East. As light was just beginning, our musical words from "The Old Rugged Cross" met a new day with warmth that took the chill away.

Six miles after our departure, we stopped for water and enjoyed a celebration. We had made it halfway. It was eight forty-one in the morning of May 13. We had already done what most had predicted we would never do. A line was painted across the roadway, plus all the way across the interstate. It's located eighteen miles south of Balmorea, Texas, on Interstate Ten. We hugged and cried, laughed and hollered. What a feeling the wagoneers had! The excitement went on for almost an hour. I read the poem I had created just for that occasion:

> In the west Texas drylands
> Where the covered wagons go,
> We've reached another milestone
> That America will know.

Just an imaginary line
We crossed in the early morn,
Rolling into history,
Both proud and saddle-worn.

Those teamsters' hands are weathered
As others were in days gone by
And forward we'll keep going
Toward the mountains in the sky.

With not a hesitation
Do we question our last goal.
For to keep these teams a rolling
Is all that we do know.

When the sun sets over Texas
On this day, we'll feel no loss,
Held together from our sunrise
When we shared the old rugged cross.

The little town of Balmorea had sent out doughnuts and coffee. It was a wonderful day for us. It was Easter Sunday, and of course there had to be the traditional egg hunt when we arrived in camp. So Garry gave his sturdiest "wagons ho!" and we rolled on toward Balmorea.

It was an oasis in the dry lands for us. The population of Balmorea is around six hundred. We had been met by twice that many people alongside the roadway on our way to town. I will always remember all the colors and smiles. Being Easter, most of our welcomers were still in their church clothes and drove out to welcome us. There was mile after mile of pretty people. Balmorea itself had so many people waiting in the town area to see the wagon train, crowds had to be separated to let the wagons pass by. I was riding in the lead wagon and remember looking out the front at Garry leading us and waiting for the police to gently move people out of the way to let us through. Two bands were playing to welcome us. We could hear Quentin McGown's voice welcoming us and telling a little about each wagon and rider as we came in front of the viewing stand.

Traveling through Balmorea, on out toward the campsite, we were really struck by the number of welcomers, for the town was only three blocks long. One of the citizens of the town had hand painted a sign to tell the wagoneers where the camp was. However, the artist misunderstood the hanging directions. The sign was to go over the top of another sign—over the top—as in cover it. There wasn't room above the existing sign to hang ours. Therefore, the wagon train camp sign was hung below the other one. This resulted in a greeting that stated "Cemetary, Wagon Train Camp." We will always laugh about that one.

The townspeople sent a hay wagon out to camp to collect the youngsters from the wagon train to participate in the Easter Egg Hunt. The community kids were waiting for ours in town. I chose to go along with the little folks to help chaperon. Little Helen Barrett, age three, and Lyle Heber, also age three, with the South Dakota Boys' Ranch, were to be my wards. It dawned on me real quickly how hard it is to keep up with this age group when you have two real good legs, not to mention me with my slow pace. First I put Helen on one side of me and Lyle on the other right in front of the pack. When the race started, I encouraged both of them to run on ahead as I could catch up. The eggs were easily visable as all hunts are for three and four year olds. Lyle started to cry and said he would not leave me because he wanted to help me. Now here's a lad that was going to be a gentleman no matter what. Little Helen was just standing close by waiting patiently for someone to do something. I felt horrible, and could not get my small hero to budge. All of the eggs were being picked up by the rest. I kept moving all the time thinking Lyle would move on out. But he wouldn't move at all. He was not going to abandon this limping redhead. I did get him over to one egg that no one else had seen. We grabbed it with force. Helen did not have one egg. By this time, the hunt was over and we had one egg for two little people. I was wishing I had not volunteered for any of it. We walked back to where everyone was gathering to get their awards, not the place I wanted to be. The situation took a turn for the better. One very nice lady made the comment about Lyle's egg looking like a prize egg. We checked, and it was. Plus a very nice gift was awarded to Helen for not finding a single egg. Then Lyle was awarded a beautiful gift for being from the farthest point in the country at the egg hunt. Helen smiled throughout the entire hunt, and Lyle stayed close by my side to help. Those kids were great. We caught the hay wagon back to camp, and I sent my wards off with Debbie Shivers to be delivered to their parents as I had to meet with my host and hostess for the night, Fred and Mildred Stroade. We had met in Eola, Texas and they were responsible for doing wonderful things for the wagon train while we stayed in Balmorea. I guested in their home that night. Again, the hot shower was fabulous and they enjoyed the stories I shared with them about the journey.

When we rolled out of camp the next morning, our route took us along the base of the Davis Mountains. It was to be a very unique day of travel for us. We traveled back country roads, through gates that had to be unlocked, and into the foothills on old roadway that had not been used for many years. A photographer's paradise was what we called it. There were no traffic jams or anyone alongside the road. We just went out through the wilds and met face to face with mother nature. What a gorgeous place she made for us out there, in the middle of nowhere. That night in camp, the committee from Balmorea came and fed us another good dinner. They also sent word that they would open up their community pool for the wagoneers to use that evening—a real treat. Fred and Mildred had worked more of their magic.

The night's camp found us in another open camp on a hillside. Before our arrival, there was nothing there but rocks and bare ground. After the wagons came in to circle, the area looked like a small city. We could see the traffic on the highway pass by and hit their brakes. Most of the truck drivers that traveled this route regularly knew nothing was built there. However, after dark, one could plainly see all the lights and camp fires. On the C.B. radios, we heard later they would ask anyone they could just where the new village came from all of the suddden.

After we went through downtown Kent, Texas, population seventeen, we pulled into a campsite alongside the railroad tracks. We were around four miles out from Kent. Pauline, head of the committee from Kent, drove into camp and asked where she could set up some tables to bring a couple of things the wagoneers might like. I told her I would keep an eye on the open area in front of the office truck so she could return to that point to set up. Most everyone ate in their own camps, then milled around visiting. Then, from the entrance to our camp, came a line of cars through the dusty roadway. They pulled up to the previously spotted place. Pauline and her volunteers had delivered to camp every kind of homemade cookie and cake anyone could think of. They were made from kitchens with kind loving hands throughout the area. The people set up tables, eating utencils, and plates. The pastries just kept coming; we could not help but stare at such an assortment of goodies. Then we knew this dry piece of land was really an oasis lost somewhere in time. Gallons and gallons of ice cream were brought out for our eating pleasure. Every one of the wagoneers took a plate and proceeded to stack chocolate, vanilla, more chocolate, and other flavors of cakes and cookies. We took all we wanted—heaps of calories. It was fabulous. Ice cream was piled high on the plates, too. What a dessert binge we went on. To the pleasure of all the nice people that had brought it to us, we gourged ourselves silly. We leaned against trucks, trailers, our portable stage, sat on the ground, whatever it took to get this royal treat into us, we did. Pauline had also found a very good band that played as we ate ourselves sick. For those that could, an impromptu dance started up. The dance floor left a little to be desired. But then again, we had become used to sharing the floor with one another as well as rocks, mud puddles, mesquite bushes, holes, jackrabbits, and usually a very noticeable slant. None of these ever discouraged the wagoneers from dancing.

Ed and Mary Miller received bad news from home at camp at about the same time all of the entertainment started. They had been with us since we left Sulphur Springs. Ed rode every day and Mary always kept the camp set up for her husband from town to town. Their home had been destroyed in Kansas and they were needed there by their daughter. They would leave immediately. We said our tearful parting words and wished them well. They did make it back before the end of the trail.

I was still staying with Suzanne Whitfield and decided to return to camp. Stopping by the office to check for any mail, I visited with Vickie Barrett as she was nearing the end of her work day. Quentin McGown was there too, but left shortly after I walked in. Quentin always remained composed when trouble was around, so it was hard to tell when a situation was urgent or not and how urgent. He opened the office door soon after he stepped out and said there was a problem outside. I knew it was serious because he slammed the door. I jumped up and threw open the door to see what appeared to be the complete Morrison Milling wagons going up in flames. I could see the babies and was so afraid they were in grave danger. I came down off of the steps, screaming, "Fire, fire, fire!" I could not run real fast, but it wasn't that far to the flames. People were coming from everywhere to help. It was very dark and near-panic filled me as I could see the babies and couldn't get there as fast as I wanted to. Suddenly, I caught a glimpse of movement to my left. It happened so fast I could not change a step. I was knocked to the ground by a football-like tackle from someone out of the dark trying to get to the fire to help also. From the glow of the flames still a ways off, I could tell it was a man with something in his hand. He fell in his efforts to miss me. We both went tumbling to the ground. I jumped up and he was up and gone as quicky as he came, off into the dark to help. I had no idea who it was. Rushing toward the wagons, I grabbed the little ones and got them away from the flames. One wagoneer ran up to the flames, threw the bucket of water he had, missed the entire blaze and all, but drowned three men fighting the flames with crude tools. We did not qualify for any volunteer fire department anywhere in the world, but we sure kept trying. So many came with buckets of water, the flames were finally extinguished. Though the train was usually camped out in a dry area away from any facility that would handle emergencies, the wagoneers always seemed to get the job done. From where so many came to help so quickly is a mystery but that was how the pioneers of the eighties always were when something was needed to aid another. The flames had come from an attempt to start a camp fire. We kidded Fred and David Shivers. We told them if they wanted company, just ask. We would all be glad to stop by. Burning down camp wasn't necessary!

After ninety-two days on the road and many memories, we were still going strong, ready to challenge anything in the pathway. Wagoneers came and went. We continued out across the hot dry lands of west Texas, crossing some places that we were told had not seen rain since 1959. It showed, too. The attitude of the residents of that part of the state were all very good. I cannot tell anyone why, just that it took this kind of a person to settle that part of Texas and it was passed on down through generations. I still took my walks across camp to watch the life seep into the circle of wagons. I would watch the horses and mules led out into the center to be harnessed or hooked up to each wagon. The cool of these mornings always found the stock and their handlers feeling ready to go. Dust was kicked up all around and the sun's rays shone through to light up each canvas as if it were a large lamp.

The pioneers of the eighties always greeted one another each new day as if they had not seen the other for a long time. These greetings were always infectious. Warmth and affection mixed with admiration and respect were always the tone of the day. Garry France gave us more than one thousand "wagons ho!" as we came around the state, and we never got tired of hearing it or listening for the voice. What a sound! The stock also knew and pricked their ears as Garry raised out of his saddle each time to call us on.

Chapter Fifty-three

Out of more than fifteen hundred committee members around the state who oversaw so many details when the wagon train came to their areas, one name came to mind often: Mrs. Noble Smith of Van Horn. She was blessed with an abundance of energy, surpassing at most just one-fourth of her eighty-two years. She stood not quite five feet tall, but cast a shadow longer than one could measure. She was the head of the Sesquicentennial Committee for Culberson County and handled everyone with dignity and pride. Due to doubling back from El Paso along the north side of the state, we would be staying in her county more nights than any other county in the state. I believe Mrs. Smith was more proud of that than anything. She lives in Van Horn and our visit and stay in her area was very pleasant. Unfortunately, Mrs. Smith was ill with the flu while we guested in her town, but it didn't dampen her spirit. She was a trouper all the way. I was very glad the wagon train had a layover day in Van Horn for us of course, but most of all, for Mrs. Smith to see the fruits of her labor come to life. There were talent shows, wonderful food, and hospitality beyond belief.

When I took my early morning walk around camp on the second day in Van Horn, little Lyle, my protector from the Easter Egg Hunt, fell in beside me. He had on his usual big cowboy hat. One always had to look twice to see if there was really anyone under the moving hat, for Lyle was dwarfed by it. He stuck his hands in his pockets and told me about the happenings of the night such as the new foal that had come to us in the wee hours of the morning. He warned me of the oncoming water truck, so as not to get wet when it passed by. Also, we were to be on the lookout for his dad, Rusty. Lyle had to see him. All of the important things to a three year old in the early morning hours. Lyle spotted his father and bolted in his direction. The school bus with our students was just leaving camp at the end of my walk. I waved to all and turned to face another day of activity for a wagoneer.

That evening Quentin and Laurie McGown urged me to stay in their motor home. They were staying in town and knew how sick I had been the last few days. My flu bug was visiting again. I accepted for two reasons. The first, I could rest undisturbed and needed it. Secondly, their quarters were like the Hilton!

Chapter Fifty-four

The dry lands were beginning to take their toll on the pioneers of the train. Between flu, shortage of money, and sick animals, more had to quit and go home. For those of us who stayed, we would miss them very much, but again we were reminded of a century ago when the first settlers would run out of supplies or food or water or money. It must have been sheer hell to give up a dream or a goal that they put their souls into, only to fall short of the fulfillment of it. Just because we live in the twentieth century does not mean that we did not feel the impact of sudden awareness of goals not reached. Time did not erase the heartbreak of not going all the way, whether it be now or then. We were all out there to do the same thing. We could help one another as much as we could, but the odds were against some of them. Try as we may, to take everyone just couldn't be. It was not always money or supplies that kept the wagoneers going. Sometimes it meant sitting down with them and listening to feelings of loneliness from being separated from families, or loved ones at home; it is true no one was forced out there, but we still had feelings. Even if an individual goes from their home to work, there are some days that individual does not want to go. Fortunately for us on the trail, this feeling of melancholy was spotted immediately and someone would always catch the victim and spend a moment to let them know their feelings were fully understood. Just another wonderful development shared among the pioneers.

During these west Texas days of travel, we tried to sing more often along the roadways and get everyone involved, whatever it took. Sometimes at its best, this was to be the most stressful situation anyone, anywhere could ever take on and see through to the very end. In just a heartbeat, impatience could surface, but the rock-bottom true foundation of the wagon train would not give in.

Chapter Fifty-five

In Serra Blanca, I walked into the heart of the tiny historic town. This town that had brought the two great railroads together a century before.

I had spotted an old building when we came onto the main street earlier. It was the Old Palace Hotel and Saloon. To see that old building, the name was most appropriate. The Palace had been at its height when the railroads met here a long time ago. The structure was unchanged. Leaning against the corner, I could truly hear the old piano playing, and laughter coming from within. It never takes much of an imagination when the setting is like that one was.

Since the wagon train had left Van Horn, we were starting to hear that we could not get the wagons up the

Guadalupe Mountains. We heard it everywhere. No team of horses or mules had ever pulled a wagon up this road and there sure weren't going to be very many encouraging words for us. We had visions of the roadway up the mountain being straight up. It was a public road, so just how steep could it be? Actually, we could see El Capitan reaching for the sky, way in the background from where we traveled more than two weeks in advance. We drew closer, always keeping an eye on that peak. Questions went through our minds. Some wagoneers spoke of it, some just watched that ever looming mountain top. Nothing had stopped the train by that point and it was unlikely El Capitan could. The unknown can give one second thoughts, however.

Chapter Fifty-six

When we left Balmorhea, I was going to be back in the saddle again. I had not been back to a doctor since the accident. I did remember him telling me something that stuck in my thoughts. When I felt I could get back in the saddle again, he asked me to make myself wait two weeks. So I convinced myself that the medical doctor with the degree might have a little more sense than me, out there blazing the trail in Cowtown. Therefore, I climbed back into a wagon and continued to drive and ride along. At the same time, I was on a countdown. When we left El Paso, I was going to be back in the saddle. The winds blew constantly. The flu and hard conditions going down the road made a lot of the wagoneers want to leave and rejoin at another point. All we could do was take one more step, know we had pulled one more mile, and try to keep going. It was the hardest part of the entire journey. No one said

it was going to easy. I know it crossed most everyone's mind: "How could they keep going under such conditions?"

We came to terms with the fact that our forefathers did this and were not as well off as we were. At their time in history, they did not know of invented luxuries as we do. But to make this commitment and stick it out became an obsession at this part of the trek. One needed perseverance and dedication with a large dose of inner pride and strength. It took this then, and it took it when we were there. The wagon train kept going and I have nothing but understanding for everyone who stayed and everyone that left. A wise person knows his limits no matter which side of the fence he lives on. Sometimes an individual would think of an activity to divert attentions. Pat West drove out to meet the train at a water stop and played old, old country music. We all ended up singing or just sitting in the saddle listening to voices of famous cowboy tunes of days gone by.

After the wagons came down out of the foothills of the Davis Mountains, the Rio Grande was close by. Knowing how close the famous river was, built a new excitement amongst the wagoneers. Many went to see the river of history, to walk across or just stand and watch it flow by. The Rio Grande has changed its pathway many times in the course of years, sometimes much to the anguish of the ranchers and farmers along the river banks.

From the campsite at Fort Quitman, we did get a taste of the once mighty river. Because of international laws, we had to be away from the banks by sundown, but no one caused any problem with this.

Coming into Fort Quitman, we did not hear favorable reports about the camp. However, upon arrival, we were pleasantly surprised. It was dry, but then we were still in west Texas and it was dusty. The community had provided

a water truck that continuously kept a driver working to keep the dust to a minimum in camp.

The border patrol was our constant companion. As we paralleled the Rio Grande. After a while, we became accustomed to seeing the green four wheel drive vehicles in camp and patrolling all hours of the night. At least we were being watched over.

I drove Miss Hazel's wagon all day coming into Fort Hancock; some of the way I was in the driver's seat alone. I felt like I had graduated; it sure felt good. The community of Fort Hancock turned out in force to greet us, entertain us, and host us in another grand fashion.

Our talent show included J.R. the sign painter, and singing renditions from old Hank Thompson and Ernest Tubb hits. Johnny Adams sang Marty Robbins favorites that made us want to close our eyes and just see Marty standing there. Marge and Charlie Campbell, Suzanne Whitfield, and even Garry did a song he wrote for Jan. The spectators were just as enthusiastic as the entertainers. A wonderful time was had by everyone in that tiny town.

The next day was our layover day, so A. D. Parks, Pam Blanscet, Mike McGuffy, Shelly, Joany, Billie Montgomery, and I all took five head of horses, six cameras and a few cold drinks to the Rio Grande to ride across. I think someone said John Wayne did it once. Well, that sure made it the thing to do then. We pulled up to the edge of the water and prepared to make the crossing into another country. I was going to ride out of El Paso, but had not ridden since the accident, therefore I volunteered to photograph the program. A. D. and Mike were in the water first, they rode across and waved back at me. I ended up with four cameras to man. Everyone didn't know I was just a backyard photographer. Mike and his mount rode out to the middle, A. D. came charging at him, water flew everywhere, and there was laughter in the air. It became quite a game. Pam got involved and so did Shelly and Billie. Everyone paired up, rode out to the midle of the river, turned, paced off about one hundred yards, then raced toward one another as fast as they could. The water was like a curtain; I could barely make out each rider by the time they met to touch hands when they passed. Their free feelings were contagious. I took many pictures and loved my viewpoint. Afterwards, A. D. asked me if I wanted to ride his horse across the river to Mexico just to say I did it. Pam offered to stay close by. I knew nothing could be safer. After all, they had already ridden the fire out of the horses, and I could see there weren't any holes. I rode to the middle turned in the saddle to wave to A. D., since he was recording this with my camera, then rode on across to the other side. Pam and I posed again. We started back carefully. I was struck by the idea suddenly, why not? I stuck my heels in that horse and we came across that river as fast as I could urge him on. With usual caution to the wind, we went for it. Grabbing the saddlehorn, I could see the bank coming up on us quickly through the curtain of water that surrounded us. I just urged the animal on more with a flying leap, soaking wet, and what felt like half of the water in the Rio Grande. We came out of Mexico and the river just like someone said John Wayne must have done at least a dozen times. The photo shows the exact feeling I had when that horse and I made that final jump up and out. Just then a border patrol officer came up and asked us a few questions. We had finished the games and were unsaddling the stock to cool them down. We invited him and his family to join us on the train up the Guadalupe Mountain and he in turn gave each of us an official border patrol patch. We had a lot of fun with them later.

Fort Hancock had an excellent restaurant that quickly

became a favorite spot for us. O. J.'s had food that we had not tasted since most of us left home many weeks before. A message was sent to our camp the first night that the little café would be kept open for us later than the regular hours. We piled into pickup trucks, cars, and some even walked. Jan and I chose to order a banana split. Being late at night and in the dry lands, it sounded like the perfect idea. Our banana splits were not a disappointment; we were served a huge dish of at least five thousand calories. All of a sudden, many people in the room thought our splits were the best thing also. I am not one to share a dessert I've ridden ninety-nine days to get and neither was Jan. We armed ourselves with forks in our left hands to ward off extra hands reaching for our treat and proceeded to enjoy the sinfully delicious bowl of goodness with the right. I will add there were some wounds inflected—a prime example of adult behavior in a public place.

Fort Hancock has an old church. I always went to these serene old buildings as often as I could along the trail. The small towns and communities along the border of Old Mexico seemed to preserve their parish halls to the theme of the old. Getting down on the prayer bones and thanking the lord for bringing us one more day, one more mile, safely and still going, was necessary, I felt. I slipped into the church and was met by seven people of the community. The small gathering consisted of women dressed properly. I, of course, always wore my traveling clothes from the trail. I quietly excused myself from their presence as I could return later. They wouldn't hear of it. Stepping aside, they sat quietly on the benches as I walked toward the altar and knelt. I did not look over my shoulder, but completing my personal words, I turned to leave and was met full face by the little group I had interrupted. They approached me to thank me for coming and sharing their church. Again they stepped back out of the aisle to have me pass by and exit the church. It was a strange warm feeling I had from the group of worshippers—like a weary traveler being welcomed into the fold of strangers, but not being treated as a stranger. I waved to them as I drove away and they returned my gesture.

We left Fort Hancock after a nice two-day stay behind us. The girls from O.J.'s restaurant came out to wave us farewell as we passed our favorite little spot on the way out of town. We were fifty-seven miles from El Paso—fifty-seven miles from my saddle.

Chapter Fifty-seven

April tenth was spent in Tornillo. I was very blue on that day as it was my anniversary. I knew I would not see Bobby and this date only made me feel more lonesome. I had written him a poem that I hoped he would get in time. A phone call later might help, but my tough exterior would give away to my ice cream heart.

At the first water stop of the day, David Shivers told me Teresa wanted to see me. I was tending to Miss Hazel's stock and said I'd be right there. I approached the Shiver's wagon and Teresa handed me a beautiful handmade greeting card. Through my tears, I thanked her for her thoughtfulness. All of the wagoneers were a very special group of folks. As I walked back up the line, Jan and Garry came up to me and said I was to go to dinner with them that evening in honor of my anniversary. They said they would take full responsibility for seeing to it that my evening was cheerful. I could not help but already be cheered with the attitude of these two couples.

Laurie McGown took me to the laundry to get the

chore out of the way, then Garry and Jan picked me up along with eleven others they included. Up on a hill overlooking the dry lands of the Rio Grande ranchlands, we had a wonderful dinner, caring friends, and loving people. I toasted to my husband, hoping he was having as good a dinner as I. Somehow I did not think so. Those fabulous people cheered me up despite my missing partner.

Chapter Fifty-eight

Crossing the El Paso county line, I was driving Miss Hazel's wagon. She was usually an endless source of wit to me. This wasn't any different. She jabbed me in the ribs with her elbow and said if I pulled the team out of line and up in front of the store sitting on the county line, jumped out and tied the mules to the pole, she would pay me ten dollars. The store was a liquor store. She said we could both run in and have a shot of "Red Eye." I almost fell out of the wagon laughing. I knew Miss Hazel did not drink, but she was going to make the best of it. She told me no one would know that we were really going to use the restroom. She is a dandy.

Tornillo sent a welcoming group of mariachis to entertain us at our lunch stop. That was a very nice change of pace. Entertainment in the middle of the highway. Bert Payne found a partner and danced in the roadway.

Closer to town, we were met by two wagons pulled by horses carrying signs welcoming us to the community. Another west Texas greeting—warmth everywhere, and plenty of it. Tornillo treated us as if we were long lost citizens of the town coming home.

Since the beginning of the journey, we all had been most concerned about the safety of the people that always walked among us in camp, at water breaks, or anywhere we stopped. Many children would walk so close to the animals. Trying to educate their parents about keeping a safe distance in just one twenty second lesson was next to impossible. Little hands would always be there to touch horses and mules with blinders that could not see anything but straight ahead. It appeared to us that the average visitor thought if we could take this event down the road with everything we had around us, then it must be safe to reach and touch the animals at any given point. They were unaware of the continuous eye we had to keep on the livestock just to make sure nothing happened.

We rolled into Fabens, a small community on the Rio Grande, south of El Paso, and made the turn to go by the schools as we had done throughout the trip. This time we were greeted by two thousand students from the kindergarten class right up to the seniors in high school. The majority held a small Texas flag to greet us as we passed by. There were bright colored signs to welcome the wagoneers. This journey was made for the young and the old, and they turned out in force in Fabens. More future leaders watching the wagon train showed them where their roots and heritage came from. We stopped right in front of the schools. Our first thought was of their safety, never had we stopped anywhere between so many children, and with all of them standing just a few feet from the animals. Apparently they had been told not to do anything to start trouble, and whoever told them put it in such a way that not one young person broke that rule. We admired them for this control. I was asked to speak to the students of the high school history class and share the experiences of the trail. It was the least I could do to show our appreciation for their conduct. Also, many of the students walked amongst us serving cold drinks and homemade cookies.

Mike Lowery, our resident trick roper, brought his horse, Cash, out in front of the students and performed many of his tricks for the students. They loved it as we all did. He stood in the saddle and brought the old west show to them as they would never see again.

The wagons rolled out of town toward camp about ten. I stayed at the school until the end of the school day. The students were a captive audience and responded on their own accord when I turned the questions over to them. Fabens has a marvelous student body. I was very proud to have had the opportunity to share our trip with them, thanks to Coach Scott.

Chapter Fifty-nine

El Paso, our westernmost point of travel around the state was also a major accomplishment for the wagon train. We would stay three nights and enjoy many hospitalities.

One more stop, however, was to be made before reaching El Paso: San Elizario. Greeted by everyone that lives in San Eli, a natural high kept a smile on everyone's face and warmth in our hearts. A big celebration was held in our honor and excitement was mounting for us.

The route from San Eli to El Paso was lined with welcomers. Our water stop was especially nice. An old mission in Socorro was to be the setting. Just as we entered the parking lot of the mission, someone rang the bells in the belfry, bringing another tear as always. Something about the bells and a wagon train symbolized our ancestors.

A large crowd of townspeople were there to see that we received refreshments and the attention we needed and to let us know they were proud that we had made it to them.

My gypsy existence and scattered belongings all over camp still did not change my attitude toward traveling the entire state in search of an answer as to how a foundation was made by determined people a long time ago.

Just as we entered El Paso I put these words together about our arrival into the area:

> In Socorro where the bells rang
> Just alongside Old Mexico,
> We cheered and cheered
> When we reached the edge of El Paso.
>
> Our horses, mules, the travelers
> Will rest for these three nights.
> We'll visit into Juarez,
> Come back by city lights.
>
> We've come miles across this Texas
> Met by dust and heat and wind.
> If you ask all the weary people,
> We'd do every mile again.
>
> Here at the base of the mountains
> And the entrance to another land,
> The canvas tops are waiting
> To turn back home again.
>
> Seventeen hundred miles
> Of outstretched hands have touched us.
> We're a fine-tuned guitar playing
> Or the Yellow Rose of Texas.

How do we just keep going?
So many seem to ask.
We pray that they can see
The light we're carrying from the past.

I was still feeling a little blue due to the absence of
Bobby. I had called him that day before we pulled into El
Paso. He seemed to be suffering the same melancholy I
was.

Our first morning in El Paso found the Shivers outfit
having a problem with one of their horses colicking. I went
to the barn where the animal was. Fred and David had
been up most of the night taking turns watching over the
horse to make sure the animal did not lie down, which
would result in the horse's death. Ranger weighed about
seventeen hundred pounds and we could not lift him if
he went down. Thus, the vigil.

Doctor Ken had been with the horse most of the night
to help also. Debbie and Teresa were relieving their hus-
bands. Laurie McGown and I volunteered to watch the
Shiver's little ones while the ladies went to shower. We
were inside a large covered arena and knew we had to
keep Ranger going to help him. Laurie and I were sitting
in two chairs that someone had provided for the shifts of
horse sitters that came and went throughout the time we
were in El Paso.

I glanced across the arena and noticed a man and
woman climbing over the fence. I thought briefly that the
man looked so much like Bobby, but put that thought off,
as he was six hundred miles away. However, my eyes
went back to the man helping an older woman over the
fence. I knew it was him. I could not run, but I jumped
up off the chair and hurried towards him. He turned and
sure enough, he came running toward me and as usual, I

knocked our hats off into the dirt when I hugged him tightly. Aunt Florence had come in also. I started to ask all kinds of questions. Then suddenly, Bobby told Laurie, when I introduced them, that I was going home. I could not understand. He just stated his point about how he was tired of me having all of my belongings scattered about camp and not having a place of my own. I was absolutely crushed. Asking again if everything at home was all right, he assured me it was. Therefore, I could not figure out why he kept saying I was to go home. Aunt Florence kept hugging me and I sure wouldn't be rude to her for the world, but my thoughts were racing. What about my book and everything I had been through? How could this man tell me I was to go home after so much preparation and so many sacrifices I had to make just to get this far? I did not want to cause a scene, so I thought I would wait until we were away from everyone to ask him just what in the hell the problem was. I kept introducing him to all of the wagoneers I came to. He repeated the story to each that I was going home. I wanted to scream at him to stop saying this. I wasn't going home and that was final. I had to convince him first. He wanted to go out to the car and get something. I tagged along thinking if I got him alone, I'd find out what the problem was if I didn't hit him first!

He reached into the back of the car and pointed toward the big truck and camper sitting in the next parking spot saying, "This is home." First I yelled with excitement and joy. Then I reached over and punched him in the shoulder. Then I kissed him. It was a dirty trick to play on me. At the same time I should have remembered just how mischievous my husband is. I told him he was the meanest, nicest man I knew. After driving all over camp to pick up my belongings that were literally spread out over nine locations, I pulled the camper into line right beside Suzanne

Whitfield's rig and had a permanent home for the rest of the journey. Trying to keep up with my journal every day, plus my saddle and gear for Lady, as well as the rest of my things was going to be easy.

Word spread throughout camp that I had a new home. I must have had seventy visitors the first night. It was good to know so many cared about my welfare. God love them. I would get even with my prankster husband somehow down the line.

The wagon train paraded around El Paso to honor our westernmost point. Ina Nell Wood (Woody) had worn a cap most of the journey. She had become symbolic to all of us by that hat. Along the parade route, she spotted a person in a wheelchair. Stepping out of the lead wagon, Woody gave that hat to the surprised spectator. Those of us that knew Woody realized what a gesture she was making. But Woody, always in total control of herself, would not have tolerated any recognition for her warm heartfelt thoughtfulness. So we left it alone and admired the act from afar.

Bobby, Aunt Florence, Jan, Bill Tooley, Carmelia, Bob Duffy, and a few others got together for a trip across the border to shop and have an authentic dinner in Mexico. Later, the necessary laundry and supplies were taken care of while we stayed in this border town. We knew it would be weeks and many, many miles before we had the chance to shop in the same way we could in El Paso.

Having my own camper, I stocked up and fixed my little home on wheels to suit my comforts.

On the morning of the fifteenth of April, I saddled up my mare and rode out into the circle of wagons to ride out of camp with my friends for the first time in over five hundred miles and seven and one-half weeks. As Lady and I went into the circle, many of the wagoneers cheered us and I once again felt the tears sting my eyes. I was back in the saddle again. They knew how I had missed it, and I felt very proud of all these wonderful pioneers for all of the mental and spiritual help they had sent my way while I limped along and stuck out a commitment that was more than likely the hardest commitment I would ever fufill in my entire life. They all knew how I had waited, not always with patience, to ride again. Mr. Oliver came and shook my hand and welcomed me back to the ranks of the riders again.

I rode the mare halfway to the next camp; then Joy Williams picked her up and took her on to the next camp. I caught a wagon.

Bobby and Aunt Florence had to head back to Forth Worth. They moved my camper on up to the new camp. The constant dry wind blowing and ever present dirt had made a lot of us cough and become ill again. I had falsely thought I was to escape all of the sick business again, still believing I was the invincible one.

Chapter Sixty

The Guadalupe Mountains were just a few days away. Still listening to the rumors that we could not get up the mountainside, nerves were being stretched to the ultimate. We knew we had conquered every obstacle such as this, but the maximum test was yet to come. Fred and David's horse, Ranger, had survived the attack of intestine illness, only to be bitten by a snake. He then was still not able to work until this malady was overcome. Ranger was one of the best harness horses in the Shivers' string of animals. He ultimately would recover, but it took a while. His true spirit was tested on the journey and I, for one, hope he went to a good home after being sold at the auction at the end of the trail in Forth Worth.

Our first camp out of El Paso was an open camp, as usual with no facilities. As it turned out, the next sixteen camps in a row were open camps.

We did stay on a ranch, a two days' ride from El Paso, but as I understood it, the owners were not at home during our stay. Most of the campsites were set up well over a year before the wagons ever rolled out of Sulphur Springs. Therefore, some of the camps were entered without anyone knowing we were there. As the opinion about the wagons ever making three weeks of the journey, let alone eighteen hundred miles was so prominent, it did not surprise me. We had total belief in our trek but could understand why the pessimism occurred.

Chapter Sixty-one

Cornudas, Texas is a large area of absolutely nothing. The wind blew us onto the campgrounds and never let up after we stopped.

The big peak of the Gaudalupe Mountains was only two days away. We had heard that the winds could reach over one hundred miles per hour. The pioneers had lived with all of the negative thoughts and words about taking the train up the mountains; now the day of reckoning was near. I saw many of the teamsters turn toward the peaks and just watch, and many others making sure the wagons were checked over from every aspect.

Later in our windy camp, the population around Cornudas provided us with a first class greeting. Because of the constant wind blowing, our two shuttle buses, the Purina Feed truck that always traveled with us, plus our office with the fold out stage and storage room on the back were all pulled into place to provide a break against the wind. We did not see where the people or the vehicles came from, but gathering around our carefully parked trucks, we began to see many people carrying the most wonderful dishes of food. Another stage had been set up and live music was being played to our enjoyment. We formed a line and just stood by watching. At least fifty different kinds of salads were brought out.

The food was first rate; at no other time on the trail had we been offered such a spread as this. Being out in the middle of nowhere in a dust storm ended up being a treat. A water truck had been provided to water down the area adding to our comfort. However, we had already decided that eating at home was never to be complete without a pinch of dirt and a couple of horse or mule hairs added.

When the wagons left Cornudas the next morning, the winds did not come up until later in the afternoon. Therefore, we were treated to a clear view of El Capitan, the prominent point of the Guadalupe Mountains we had watched for so many miles. To say we were two days from the mountains did not put the train very far away. The two days were as wagons travel. We were traveling in the only part of the state that did not have onlookers lined up along the roads. Now we knew how far we were from anything. It was unsual not to see a line of people, but at the same time we wouldn't have been able to present a real true welcome as the winds whipping so hard made our mouths and eyes fill with dirt. It was always better to travel with our heads down and mostly covered.

Salt Flat, Texas, very similar to Cornudas. The main difference, Salt Flat had three stores where Cornudas had one. Our main problem was no ice. Most of the wagoneers had become accustomed to storing food in ice. I had just stocked up on my provisions in El Paso, but my refrigerator only kept food with a block of ice, versus propane. My food began to spoil as well as other wagoneers'. We needed these supplies and hated to lose anything of this nature. Cotton Williams opened up his facilities to the wagoneers to use to repair their wagon wheels and wagons in preparation for the climb up the mountain. Welding and repairing went on into the night hours.

Salt Flat provided us with cakes and cookies. We should each have weighed ten or twenty pounds more instead of less, but the hard work kept things in balance. By the time the train reached this part of the state, everyone had lost weight. I wouldn't recommend to everyone to catch the next wagon train that comes past their house in order to shape up, but it will work.

I do not know how the women of a century ago ever carried buckets of water and managed to get up off the ground with them. I tried it with my long blanket that I always wore and kept stepping on it. The water splashed and I ended up wearing soggy clothes while the animal was without water until I tried it again. The pioneer women were a group of people that should be recognized much more than they are now. They had children on the trail, walked beside their men into hostile lands, and provided everything that was necessary for a wife and mother to provide along the way. Those women deserve a shrine like the Alamo to honor them.

On April nineteenth, we camped at the base of the Guadalupe Mountains. Straight up we looked; the cliffs hung above us like giant ghosts from medieval days. The trip to the base of these mountains found us looking out across dry lands that had nothing to sustain any life it seemed, but there were deer and wildlife waiting for us to pass by. Nature has an odd way of distributing living things in strange places.

Our camp was small and cramped, but we made do and just squeezed closer. As soon as the sun set over the mountaintops, a new member of the train suffered a heart attack. He was brought back to breathing once, thanks to the strong efforts of our medical people, but he slipped away again. We were over one hundred miles from the nearest medical facility. Frustration and anger was felt throughout the camp. The wagoneers were a very proud group; they felt the loss personally. Nothing could save the man, and the majority of the wagoneers did not even know the gentleman. But he was one of us and that was all that mattered.

The next morning, most of the camp was up early. The rangers reminded us that the winds could get up to over one hundred miles an hour. Some of the drivers chose to remove the canvases from their wagons. This would help save a wagon if they were caught in a crosswind. Wheels were checked again. Teams were readied for our assent up the notorious mountainside. Garry France told us we would be starting at at least forty-five yard intervals.

I cannot say there were no negative thoughts, because of all the opposing words we had heard. However, it was time to go. The hour of reckoning was upon the wagoneers. Just about the time Garry was to call "wagons ho!", I heard a commotion over my left shoulder. In turning, I saw Lloyd, one of the hands from the Dairy Queen outfit, fall to the ground. Loud screaming came from the same direction. I turned Lady and raced to see if any help was needed. I could see blood all over the place. I hollered for a medic. I did not know the problem, but it looked serious. A large piece of bloody meat lay on the ground by Lloyd. In times as this, it is almost automatic to have people rush to help or just watch. I could see our medical people running toward the downed man, and over my right shoulder, I saw a horse standing with a huge gaping hole in his left flank. I have never seen such a wound in any animal. I screamed for Dr. Ken but could see he was already on his way. Realizing the flesh was not Lloyds, I breathed more easily. It seemed a team of mules had been left unattended by a new driver. The team spooked and ran over the horse, wounding the animal very seriously. Lloyd tried to stop the runaway and was knocked down. He would be sore, but nothing permanent. The horse was a very sad story. Everyone tried to help as best they could. Some say more could have been done; I do not know. The horse was loaded into a trailer, but again we were still one hundred ten miles from any medical facility. Unfortunately, the brave animal made it to the facility, but due to a great loss of blood, he dropped in the trailer just as the truck pulled into the vet's office and died.

We would not find out about the fatality until we reached the top. It was good that we had something such as the mountain to take our minds off of this base camp.

The lead wagon left with its outrider, Tommy Underwood, riding just beside it. Miss Hazel's wagon was next. Lady and I rode alongside her with Mark Morton, as he wanted to see to it that his little mules made the trek up the moutainside in good shape with no help. Mark had a lot of pride in his Shetland mules. A lot of the teamsters told him they would never make this run. Mark felt differently. He was followed by Leo Miller in the Copenhangen/ Skoal wagon; WBAP, driven by Glynn and Winnie Pearce; the Triland's stagecoach; Morrison Milling; Wrangler; Dairy Queen; Cody Marketing; and so on down the line. The teams had never had to wait so long to leave a camp, so it was hard to hold them back. Whenever they heard Garry's "wagon's ho!" they knew it was time to roll. Not so on this day. The good Lord was watching over us once again. There was just a breath of a breeze as we traveled up. Lady became overheated so I held her back, not wanting her to get all worn out. About seven wagons passed us. She was soaked with sweat, and I couldn't calm her down. Finally she took the situation too hand. Biting the bit, she started a very slow lope up the mountainside. At first I worried, but she fought so hard to go. We passed all of the wagons that had passed us. We even caught up with Miss Hazel. I glanced down and touched her. I pinched her hide to check her recovery rate and was totally shocked to see she was dry and calm. The mare just knew what wagon she was to be next to and was not about to be left behind when this one went over the mountain top.

About 150 yards from the entrance to the campgrounds, I glanced back to see if all was well. I saw Glynn Pearce urging his team to pass Miss Hazel's wagon. Miss Hazel was not about to be outdone by anyone; she called to the little mules and they picked up the speed. Right behind both of these wagons, Leo Miller came with his four-up hitch. They were all even at one point, and Miss Hazel would not give in to another wagon being up that mountain before her. The looks on all three of the faces of those seventy years plus youngsters was a sight to behold. I was shocked. But now I don't know why. They had each passed the lead wagon way down the moun- tain. I know now they all three must have had this idea in their minds from the very beginning. I spurred my mare to keep up with them. Mark was worried about his mules; as he thought Miss Hazel might get hurt. Of all the times for a camera not to be at hand, this was it. We came into the campground full speed ahead, caution to the wind, not the safest way but I know those three were fulfilling a dream that they would never in their years be able to duplicate. That part of it, I can appreciate. Miss Hazel was seventy-eight, Mr. Pearce was the baby at seventy-two, and Leo Miller had celebrated his seventy-sixth on the trail. I will always remember the looks on their faces, when I am in my seventies I hope I can be as notty as they all were. God love them.

Our first day on the mountain was spent riding up the trails of Guadalupe Park. We had to get a permit to ride the trails. Almost all of the horseback riders participated. Laurie and Quentin came to my camp and took me to the famous Carlsbad Caverns in New Mexico, forty miles down the road. I had heard about these caverns for so many years, but to see them was an unbelievable treat. We also went back up to the cave entrance at dusk to see the bats fly out of the entrance by the thousands upon thousands—another memory. Returning to camp, we learned about Pam Blanscet riding up onto the mountainside and only her horse returning. It seems she went about four miles up, found a nice place to picnic, and got off Duke to let him graze, while she ate and dozed. Whereupon Duke chose to return to camp. Pam ended up walking back. She was safe but we didn't know it for a while.

Our three-night stay on the mountain was to include the wagon master's birthday. He loved the mountains and the route had been mapped out to allow him to be at the very top of Texas on that day. The highest point in the Guadalupes is eighty-seven hundred feet. A photographer's paradise.

On the morning of the twenty-first, we all gathered by our portable office/bandstand to have a group photo taken in honor of all of us that had made the journey up the mountain with the train. For we had proven once again that the wagon train could conquer. The wind had not blown, there had been no accidents, and we were safe. Another milestone had been met head on; the wagons were still rolling.

The twenty-second was Garry's birthday. Vern and Margaret Renz, Hogg and Helen Jones, Kyle from Triland Corporation, Garry, Kenny and Carol Taylor, and I picked out a route up the mountain and off we rode. Lady was born and raised in the flatlands of the desert, so I was aware of the dangers of taking a crazy barrel horse from the flatlands up a trail like the one we were about to climb. I decided to ride a short while, test her ability, then return if it was to much for her. About three and one half miles up the steep winding trail we stopped to watch the awesome view. One could literally see forever. Miles and miles of Texas spread before us. I dismounted to take pictures of everyone. Lady took the opportunity to return down the mountainside. I was frightened because I knew she would never make it alone. I was the only one out of my saddle. Kenny and Carol Taylor went after her. She missed the trail and went on toward another side of the mountain. Just about everyone in our group went to get her. They did it in a perfect way without frightening her. Kenny reached Lady first. I stood and did the only thing I could think of—I photographed the rescue.

We went up and over the top of that peak, down a ways, then back up another steeper trail. It was a shear drop off on one side. I couldn't have turned around to go back if I had wanted to. Up, up we rode to the base of El Capitan, a sheer rock cliff up to the point. The trail leveled a bit, and we dismounted to rest, drink cool water Helen had brought, and just sit around telling stories. I know everyone in our group will carry the memory of that moment on the mountain forever, a mountain we had been warned about so many miles back down the road. As we left, Garry stood and tipped his hat toward the cliffs stating, "Thank you El Capitan, for hosting us." It was time to return to camp. A birthday party had been planned for the wagon master.

We combined a talent show with the birthday celebration for our leader. Bob Duffy, our official sculpture for the train, presented Garry with a piece of work he had done especially for Garry—a statue of Garry sitting on his horse calling, "Wago-o-o-onn-s ho-o-o-o-o!"—a memorable pose to all of us. Kenny Taylor and Vern Renz, who spent almost the entire journey either having Garry arrested for no reason at all or causing him untold anxious moments of frustration, all in fun of course, did not let the celebration go by unnoticed. They presented a box to Garry, but first they struck the box with many holes in it, using a chain. Naturally this made anyone in the area cautious. We were all wise to Kenny and Vern's constant pranks. After a big to do with the box, they opened it and inside was a piece of leather signed by the wagoneers wishing him well on this day. Before Garry opened the gift, the look on his face was priceless. He was all to well aware of his traveling companions' mischievous behavior. It was with caution he even wanted the box opened. I am sure the thought to run off of the stage occurred to him more than once. He always remained a real trooper about those things.

I had written two poems for this day; plus Quentin had asked me to write something about the Independence Day for Texas celebrated on the previous day on the mountain.

My first piece of work I read to Garry for his special day:

> He's walked among us,
> This quiet man of strength.
> He's lead this wagon train
> And won't stop at any length.
>
> You'll see him up in front
> Or somewhere along the side,
> Always watching, riding, checking
> With brown chaps of young calf hide.

He started out a rancher,
Took this job to guide us well.
He's brought us to this mountain.
The pioneers will always tell.

About a man who rode into history,
Leading a covered wagon train
With all his faithful followers
That feel about this man the same.

He's here every single morning
As on his mount he'll take a stance,
Throw back his head to call us on,
Our wagon master, Garry France.

The second piece was in honor of all of the wagoneers
that had made it that far. I knew they would be there in
the end:

In the Guadalupe Mountains
With cliffs above us high,
We conquered this steep roadway
That stretched up towards the sky.

Just a gentle breeze did meet us
Far apart the wagons rolled.
El Capitan did greet us,
Strength came from our very souls.

The Beauty of the valley
Lay before the watchful eyes
Was payment from the master
As we looked down with muffled cries.

The lead wagon's at the finish;
Were guided with aged hands,
As over the top they came,
One woman and one man.

Yes, we came up through the mountains
Where few thought we could pass.
As a new land spread before us,
The wagoneers where safe at last.

It was not easy to write on behalf of all the wagoneers about the Independence Day for Freedom, but the majority of them gave me the go ahead to share with everyone what I had done.

I told of how we were all so very much aware of what a special day it was not only for us but for Texas, feelings that came to us from a century ago from places like the Alamo, Goliad, Gonzales, all the way to the very moment we were standing on that mountaintop. History is always growing and expanding as the wagon train continued on its journey to help everyone remember all of the historic places we were to pass, plus those we had not come to yet—every single individual that traveled down the road, the teamsters, riders, mule skinners, and everyone responsible for transporting the camp equipment forward every day. All of them had to realize how they were writing another page in history and would continue to do so until the last mile had been walked. I reflected on a handful of volunteers capturing Santa Anna in the San Jacinto Forest on that very day 150 years ago. I knew it was only fitting that right there on the mountain where the wagons were quartered that we, a handful of volunteers, pay homage to those men and everyone after them that had bought and paid for our rights and freedoms with blood, honor, dignity, and pride. The Texas Wagon Train possessed the same qualities. I asked the wagoneers to look at themselves. *Did they not feel Sam Houston would be as proud of them on that mountain as we were of him in the San Jacinto Forest so many many years earlier?* As we traveled forward from that point, as we had done for one hundred eleven days, I reminded them to travel with God, and to appreciate the careful guiding hand of those that lead us, and always remember the peace we had all paid for.

Chapter Sixty-two

Mark, our Purina truck driver, Suzanne Whitfield, Woody, Kyle Carlson, our young folks, Reka France, Cody France, Rowdy France, The Shivers Girls, and many more entertained everyone so wonderfully.

There are those I have forgotten to write about. My notes that I kept daily were stolen in the stockyards at the end of the trail. Therefore, the oversight is not intentional. I apologize to each and every one that is left out.

Chapter Sixty-three

The wagons left the mountain, traveling out into the vast quiet lands of Texas. Nothing met us; nothing was expected. Still it was a photographer's delight. Ultimately, the pictures taken in that area were to go on to be some of the most famous works taken along the trail.

As we came to the intersection close to the New Mexico border, I told Jan I was going to race across the border just to know I had been there. She asked Garry if he was going to lead everyone that wanted to go across. He looked like it was the most undignified thing anyone could ask him. She turned to me and yelled, "Okay, Donna. Let her go." I squeezed Lady with my knees and away we went. The state troopers were standing near the intersection. They called out to me that I could not ride across the border. I did not do it to defy them. I had planned on crossing that line and a plea was not going to prevent it. We crossed the state line, I threw my arm up and gave the victory yell. Riding back to take my place beside Miss Hazel's wagon, my feelings were that of exhiliration. Garry rode past me and looked as if he were going to say something to re-mprimand my behavior. Instead, he continued on to the front of the train. Throwing up his arm, he halted the wagons. Turning slowly, he rode back down the line. Just as he passed me again, he mentioned in a low voice, that he was going to leave the state. All of the riders watched him, as did the teamsters. None knew what was going on. Suddenly, I did. I raced up to Jan and told her to toss me her camera because Garry was going to race everyone to the border. Looping the cord around my neck, I spurred the mare and we were off again. Just as I turned, Garry was racing everyone to the state line. Every rider that chose was right behind him. It made me laugh. They all looked like they were in the Kentucky Derby and Mr. Wagon Master was in the lead. All of the riders circled the sign post, hollering and whooping it up. I was clicking away with the camera when a loud noise behind me made us jump out of the way. The teamsters were not about to be outdone by the horseback riders. My idea was not as un-dignified as it had seemed earlier.

Chapter Sixty-four

Our next camp on the Old Nolybeke Ranch was another wonder of trail wonders. Carlsbad, New Mexico brought us a dinner called a "Mexican Stack," a plate of special Mexican food that we were ready for. Our dining area had been provided for also, as the committee had furnished us with chairs and tables to sit down and enjoy their hospitality. That cow pasture had never looked more elegant.

Finally, we came upon the last of our open camps in numbers, in a row. We camped on the Bob Farmer land. O. C. Horn and his wife Kathryn rejoined the wagon train. Kathryn had not been with O. C. earlier, but it was good to have our old traveling friends back again.

The small towns that hosted the train in that area of Texas could not have enough said about them. The wagoneers had been out of touch with any populated area for a while. It would be time to do laundry, restock supplies, and just see a coke machine again.

The committee people of the little towns we were to travel through must have performed magic in their areas. They had dances, entertainment, meals served by smiling faces, awards given for best frontier dressed or best team or just whatever the judges could see that was unique. It was a whole new format than what we had experienced for many days in a row riding in a dust storm.

In Orla, Texas, one of the citizens of the town donated a painting of her family history to the wagon train. There were tears streaming down her face as she passed that painting on to us and told the story of how her great grandfather had settled in Orla and built his roots right into the ground. The painting was exquisite and we were proud of her for her generosity.

Fred and Mildred Stroade, of Balmorea, came to visit

me in Mentone. Those kinds of friends were made by all of us as we passed along the trail around Texas. It was most warming to have friends come to us at later points. We enjoyed a wonderful visit; they drove me to the showers at the school, where the committee people had spent a lot of money and time to accommodate the wagoneers as we stayed in their town.

Jan was awarded the most authentic-looking pioneer woman in Mentone. The funny part of the award was when they announced her as the winner, she was just about to finish chewing her food. She had washed her hair and set it in rollers, covered them with a scarf, and wore Bermuda shorts with tennis shoes and long socks, no make up, and a loose blouse. Just as the announcer said her name she mouthed the words, "Oh no," we had a good laugh, including the committee that had nominated her.

Throughout the trip, most of the towns would have a judging committee to choose who they thought was the most authentic-looking wagoneer, both in the wagons and on horseback. Many of the teamsters would display their plagues on the side of their wagons for all to know and see. To be chosen as one of the winners was truly a privilege. I can remember Bobby London and G. Roy Heifrin displayed a plate with the dates and towns they had won awards throughout the journey. Many of us would read the plate regularly to keep track of their accomplishments along the way.

While in Mentone, I received a letter from the White House. I had written to the president and Mrs. Reagan and invited them to come at some point along the trail and visit with us. I wanted to share with them the pioneers I was traveling with to make this historic journey. They very graciously declined my invitation and wished us all well.

Chapter Sixty-five

Kermit was a very special stop for some of us. We had a choice of foods to eat. This was a first for us, as it turned out any choice that was made was a good one.

Garry France had missed the day's ride out of Fort Stockton, and Vern Renz was the only participant to ride every step of the way on a horse. Garry had a plan.

Garry is the kind of a man amongst us that committed himself to this pilgrimage to the point that, bar none, nothing would stop him. He was not the only one with this feeling or else we all would not have been there.

I, along with a dozen others, watched this man go deep within himself to achieve this self-commitment because of the unfortunate accident involving Reka in Fort Stockton, where he missed that twenty-seven miles.

On April twenty-ninth, the wagon master trailered five head of horses along with some good hands to help him, back to Fort Stockton from Kermit to ride the exact pathway we had traveled without him. There was Hogg and Helen Jones, O. C. and Kathryn Horn, Carmillia, Kenny and Carol Taylor, Mark, our Purina truck driver, Vern and Margaret Renz and me.

Leaving the Fort Stockton campsite with only a breath of a breeze and the hot sun to dry his throat, mile after mile he rode on. He relayed those miles changing every three miles to rest the horses and keep going.

We saw a lonely rider out in a dusty nowhere, along an interstate highway. Remount after remount he went on. He refused water as he mind was only on each horse beneath him. To witness such an adventure in modern day times was an honor.

Dedication and inner pride are not buried as many would believe. You may have to look for the real men and women, but not far, as we saw all of this on a dusty trail deep in the heat of America.

A middle-aged man from a tough breed of Texan covered those lost miles to keep peace with himself.

The last one hundred yards, both the man and his horse raced to the finish to be welcomed and cheered by admiring friends, a bouquet of wild flowers and a sip of wine.

The old West still lived in our eyes, as long as our spirit carries on, there will always be a lonely rider out in a dusty nowhere with dedication and inner pride.

Later on that day, Garry was recognized for his accomplishment, but not without an element of surprise from his once again buddies, Kenny Taylor and Vern Renz. Earlier, when Garry was making the relay ride, unknown persons had called the county sheriff's department to complain about a rider passing over a roadway and leaving behind unwanted substances. A deputy was sent out to detain Garry and issue him a citation. At first we thought the officer was doing the act in jest, but he became very serious; then we did not know. He read the complaint but had his name wrong; Garry whirled his horse around and called over his shoulder what his proper name was and that the deputy had the wrong man, and away he raced.

At the evening ceremonies, again Garry's friends had the forthought to give him added recognition. He was arrested on the same charges, this time with the aid of the mayor. Garry also ended up in handcuffs again. Fortunately he was always exceptionally good natured about those pranks. Good thing, as Kenny and Vern never tired of mischievous ideas.

Chapter Sixty-six

We looked forward to the Midland/Odessa area with great anticipation, mainly for the shopping in modern stores and laundromats of larger facilities. This kind of attitude brought us all back to the present-day living and out of the original pioneer days and what those people did not have. A virtual sea of oil wells met us just outside of Odessa. For as far as the eye could see, the bobbing heads of the pumps, pulling the crude from the ground watched over us for days and mile after mile.

We camped at Notrees the night before Odessa. I knew Bobby was coming that time as I had talked with him the day before. All day long I kept expecting to see him alongside the roadway or on top of a fencepost somewhere. I never really knew about him. After arriving in camp, going back to get my camper and carefully selecting a campsite up on the hill so as to be easily found, I settled in to wait for my husband. Around ten o'clock, I found Lady to be very sick. I went to get the vet. Dr. Ken was also sick with our famous flu, so his assistant came to check Lady and see what the problem might be. The mare had a serious touch of the flu, so the vet had to be disturbed. I felt as bad for him as I did Lady, I knew he had been kicked seriously by a horse two days earlier also, but Lady was in trouble. Dr. Ken was always a trouper. I returned to my camp to wait, and two pair of headlights came up behind me. Bobby had finally made it. I was excited to see him but the welcome was overshadowed by the sick horse. At least I didn't knock his hat off that time.

Coming into Odessa, the wagon train had to pass through a rain storm. In fact we were soaked twice that day. A wind blew, not hard but steady, this dried our clothes quickly.

George Fletcher, the outrider for Morrison Milling, resided in Odessa. Garry was real good about asking the travelers from areas and towns we rode through to ride to the front of the train with him and help lead the pioneers of the 80s into their towns. George had ridden with us all the way on his long time pet, twenty-two year old "General." George rode proudly beside the wagon master, bringing the entourage into his hometown. Jackie Fletcher, his wife, had gathered together some of their friends into a yard we passed and represented a wonderful welcome for George and General. All of this took place in a driving rain storm.

Lightning flashed and the rain came down in torrents, yet we rolled right through the most wet day of the journey. We did not mind. It had been a long time since the only greeting we had was dirt, dust, and more dirt. I, along with others, didn't even bother to put on rain gear. The temperature was warm and cloths would dry quickly. They did, and it rained again. We still didn't care.

Odessa was a two-day stop. Suzanne and I had our campers backed up to one another and built a good porch. Thousands of people were in our camp this time. It looked like the public was going to catch up for not being along the roadway for days and days in a row. I sat down and created another poem for the area:

> Thunder and lightning
> Raindrops and cheers,
> Odessa did greet
> The tired pioneers
>
> We've come two thousand miles
> To honor our past,
> Down from the mountains,
> We're home bound at last.

This man and his woman
Have brought us this far,
They're reaching toward us
Like two bright shining stars.

Rivers and dry lands,
We've been through it all.
As the strong Texas flag,
We're here standing tall.

Reach out and touch us,
We're proud to be here.
Remember us, friends,
With a smile or a tear.

Two area ranchers, John and Bob Midkiff, joined the wagon train for a while in the Odessa area. I had ridden up at the front of the wagon train, alongside, and now wanted to travel a ways back. Bob and John had their wagon very near the end; it was not only a good change of pace, but I was able to make more friends from another area of the train.

Two miles out from the Odessa camp, we crossed the second one-thousand-mile line. This milestone was just as important as the first. Some of our wagoneers from earlier in the journey came just to see us cross the line. They were holding up signs and cheering us on. There were local citizens, welcomers, and all that knew of our accomplishment, including our ever present news media and enthusiastic folks from all over the world.

Alongside a monument halfway between Midland and Odessa, we stopped to celebrate amongst ourselves with more hugs and laughter. This was a brotherhood shared by all, companions through it all. The traditional tears fell on cheeks of pride and from hearts of glory. Without a doubt, the Texas Wagon Train was going to make it all the way if it took just one horseman leading the last lame animal into the stockyards staggering with a Texas flag in one hand, coaxing that same animal with the other.

Charles Oliver asked me if I had written something for the occasion, and I had:

> The Pecos the Brazos
> The old Rio Grande
> We've crossed two thousand miles
> Of this vast Texas land.
>
> Horses and Mules
> Have pulled us this far.
> Everyone in America
> Knows just who we are.
>
> No rich man or poor man
> We're treated the same
> With such smiles to enfold us
> The're proud that we came
>
> A gift of such labor
> Is unmatched in this land,
> From the gulf on the border
> To the Red River sand.
>
> Forty-seven wagons
> Are coming on strong
> In from the prairies
> We'll be home before long.

Midland was waiting for the wagon train with a wave of welcomers that seemed awesome. Odessa had provided us with an excellent dinner served by a catering service.

In Midland at the Claydesta Center the same huge number of visitors were there, too.

Also, our early morning breakfast was served by volunteers that managed to smile and welcome us even though we knew very few of them were ever up at that hour. They were great.

Our journey was taking us into the panhandle and the farm lands. No longer did we see dust storms and sand everywhere. There were feedlots, ranches, and a whole new scenic treasure spread before us.

Leaving Claydesta Center behind, the wagons were gearing up with a change of attitude once again.

The wave of the wagoneers' emotions took another swing. Dust in our clothing and belongings continuously had been a hard thing to come to terms with on a twenty-four hour basis. We had persevered and once again been the victor. Now it was time to bask in our victory of hardiness well earned.

Chapter Sixty-seven

It came as it must have 150 years ago, out of nowhere. A tribe of Indians swooped down on the unprepared wagon train, its riders, and the teamsters. I was in front alongside of Miss Hazel's wagon, riding scout. All of a sudden, I caught a glimpse of the Indians coming over a slope from behind the mesquite bushes. Our teams had been through a lot but nothing to prepare them for an Indian raid. The first team, somewhere back down the wagons, spooked and the rest followed suit. Complete pandamonium immediately hit the wagon train. My mare wanted to run the other way as far as she could from the frightening noises. Miss Hazel's team of mules took off up the bar ditch as did just about every team on the train. Some went up the middle of the road, some into the ditch on the opposite side of the highway. Total confusion was all anyone could hear: yelling and screaming from the unwelcome attackers, and us frantically trying to keep someone or the livestock from getting killed or both. I did not have time to look over my shoulder after my first glance at the original sudden noises. Lady jumped almost right out from under me. Tommy Underwood was beside the lead wagon. I flashed in my mind the accident at the base of the Guadalupe Mountains when the team spooked and ran over the horse that died. Tommy was in the line of danger and with all the noise and confusion, I could not get his attention. I called out to him to get out of the way. He could not hear, as he was trying to calm animals too. I yelled louder. There was still no response, so I screamed. He was ten inches in front of Miss Hazel's frightened team. Tommy was trailwise enough not to look back to see what the problem was. He just dug in the spurs and jumped out of the way. I managed to get Lady over to the team and grab the lines to help slow them down. Miss Hazel had them almost back to a fast walk. My voice was familiar to the team, which helped also. Lady was a mess. She couldn't accept those Indians. Frankly, I couldn't either. Fred Shivers told me later his two leaders turned around and looked straight at him in the driver's seat. That didn't work as the three wheelers were ready to run from the yelling intruders. Fred did some quick action and fast thinking to get them to all go in the same direction.

All of the teamsters proved themselves that day a first rate job of saving themselves and their teams. It came to light that our original settlers must have been through the same experiences as us, only they lost their lives. It was most obvious why. One cannot fight a runaway team and shoot too. Many lives had to have been lost with those tactics. We were angry also because of the danger to our wagoneers. The rest of the afternoon was spent keeping an eye out for a return visit from our renegade war party. We had a plan of counterattack if they showed their war paint again. They hopefully realized their actions were not conducive to our safety. One hundred fifty years did not erase the dangers of Indians on the frontier trails for a wagon train.

A short while later, we pulled up again. This time for one of the escort patrolmen to kill a large rattler. We would be in for a lot of this type of action as the days rolled by. We were in rattler country and spring was coming on.

That night was spent in a quiet open camp before traveling on to Patricia the following day.

Chapter Sixty-eight

Miles and miles of Texas, farmlands, ranchlands—it was beautiful. North was our favorite direction to travel. In the morning, the sun rose to our right and did not blind us. At noon, it was overhead but still not blinding. By evening, the sunsets were fantastic to our left, and still not disturbing to our forward direction. The winds came up in Patricia with threats of rain as dark clouds, holding the rumble of thunder within their puffy centers, passed by. We prepared for the worst but it skirted around us. Homemade ice cream, a delicious meal, was served. There was entertainment; music was heard throughout camp. Wagoneers were working into the late night hours by fire light, repairing whatever was necessary for the wagons to keep taking that one more step, one more turn of the wheel.

The small areas in Texas we passed through never

knew how much we cared about them. Their plans for the train, their many hours of volunteer work, did not go on unnoticed. It was just that getting an event further each day meant working late into dark hours in order to continue. Let me say this to each of the committee members and volunteers across this state: We loved you for your time and will always be grateful in our hearts for the untold sacrifices you made to get the wagon train down the road, too.

Chapter Sixty-nine

Lamesa, Texas, sits as an oasis would in an open land surrounded by millions of acres of farm and ranch lands. There are green trees and a carpet of lawn to walk upon for two days plus limbs touching over our heads to enfold us as a mother does a child. We camped, cradled in mother nature's embrace for those two nights and three days. We had dinner, a dance, a rodeo, carnival, breakfast, and just good old fashion hospitality that had met us everywhere.

The second branding of the wagon train brand took place there also. Kenny Taylor did the honors. Now the second symbolic mark of our journey was displayed with great pride.

The welcoming sign into the campgrounds was especially eye-catching. It simply stated WELCOME SIQUIS-SENNTENIAL—OR HOWEVER YOU SPELL IT, WAGON TRAIN. *Sesquicentennial* was the word that seemed to be the hardest to pronounce and very hard to spell throughout the trip. Many times we heard, "I'll be glad to see the end of this year so I don't have to try to say that word any longer." If only those folks could have heard any one of us try to say *sesquicentennial* at first.

I rode into Tahoka with Miss Hazel. An elderly man was picked up at the outskirts of town. H. J. Howell was helped into the lead wagon and promptly took the lines from Jan. He said he would take the team on into camp. I was driving the second wagon and our visiting riders were the son, grandson, and greatgrandson of our now lead wagon driver. Our guests told us tales about the patriarch in the lead wagon. Jan told me later her new driver took the lines with the utmost professionalism. Not surprising, his job in the days gone by was driving freight wagons from Big Spring, Texas to Tahoka. He had not picked up a set of lines in over forty years, but obviously had not lost his touch, even at the age of ninety-nine years, four months, and eight days. We were traveling with one of America's pioneers.

Chapter Seventy

Shortly after arriving in camp, James Simmons rushed by my campsite, leading his mules, still in harness. He called back over his shoulder that the wagon train had not received word in time about the old folks home that was waiting for us across town. James was getting together as many of the wagoneers as possible to go to the home. The residents were waiting for us. I ran back, saddled my mare, and rushed out to spread the word. The majority of the wagoneers had already settled in or went back to the old camp to bring their support vehicles up. Seven wagons and fifteen outriders were ready to roll in a very short time. We had no order to follow, just whomever was in line. The wagon master did join us but chose to ride shotgun beside Rudi Nelson on the stagecoach. Our police escort was waiting for us to help cross the three miles to the home through town. I volunteered to lead the group. Lady and I moved the wagons out of camp on toward our waiting special guests. James Simmons's wagon was right behind me along with all the rest of our little group. When we came around the corner to the home, I rode up and asked the officer if we could possibly take the wagons right up to the entrance of the home where the residents were waiting. He was most cooperative and led us right into the parking lot. The senior citizens welcomed our group with applause and cheers. Dismounting, we went to speak to each of the men and women that had waited so patiently for us. They were a wonderful sight, asking questions and reaching out to us. Someone from inside the home sent out fresh homemade cookies and drinks. We were served the offerings on trays, as the nurses and other personnel walked among us to give a brief history of every resident there to greet us. The youngest, an aunt of an employee, had just turned ninety-two. Another old gentleman was talking to Garry about a friend of his that he had grown up with, H. J. Howell. He wanted to know if the wagon master might know him. We all knew his friend; he had driven the lead wagon into camp that very day. The old timer asked Garry to send his best wishes. One of the nurses stepped up to let us know our curious old timer was one hundred and four years old.

We stayed a few more minutes, then had to leave. Our new friends must have thanked each and everyone of us four times apiece for coming to them to share our event. We were very moved by them. Actually it had worked out for the better; the main body of our train would never have stopped to visit with them because of the size.

I called out to make sure everyone was ready. I stepped into the saddle, threw back my head, and gave the biggest "wagons ho!" I could.

James Simmons and I had started a ritual long before

that day; we would bow to one another each time we greeted no matter where we were. Upon reaching the town square, I pulled Lady around and looked right at James and bowed in the saddle. He stood and returned the same. Laughing we turned the corner and went back to camp.

Chapter Seventy-one

In Lubbock, we circled the wagons in a field. The military was quartered on a hill off to our right as we came into camp. We were not in the safest area in town, but it felt like it with them there.

From another town, we were privileged to hear that night at our program of their plans and excitement over us coming to them. It was a good feeling to hear those words; we had listened to so many phrases of not being able to do this great event. The pendulum had now swung the other way. Just as we rolled into camp, Mr. and Mrs. Al Walker were standing there to greet each wagon and horse back rider. We had not seen them since Mr. Walker left us in Eden, and Mrs. Walker, of course, since she had fallen just outside of Kerrville. Mrs. Walker looked fabulous. She had written to me just a couple of weeks earlier with no mention of their surprise visit. What a wonderful surprise!

Our next traveling day was thirty-eight miles. I did not know we were to travel that distance or would have made different arrangements such as ride halfway and have the mare trailered in. Then I would have caught a wagon the rest of the day. I had learned earlier that I could not ride that far after the accident. Levelland may as well have been one hundred miles.

However, the rewards always outnumbered the

punishment. Arriving in camp finally, the lead wagon was stopped just outside of the wagon circle area. A lone girl was helped aboard. Jan called me up and introduced me to a young woman named Sharri. I could tell she was blind, and Jan also told me she was terminally ill with cancer. I greeted Sharri and welcomed her to our group. Many people were alongside the route we were taking around the field to circle the train. I let out my usual "Yeeeeeeeeee-Haaaaaaaaa!" Sharri copied me. It was something that made me forget my leg that was throbbing intensely. All around the field she and I did the same thing. Sharri loved the excitement of the short but fun ride. I reached out to touch her and she grabbed my hand. I wanted to thank her for being a part of our outfit. She was glowing with gratitude. I turned the mare away to find camp. My leg was as bad as it could be, but not as bad as the lump in my throat for Sharri.

The college campus where we were quartered was providing us with the night's meal—chicken-fried steak with all the trimmings. To us, it was a gourmet meal. Every one of the wagoneers walked into the carpeted, clean, pretty room and did the same thing. They looked up and around, picked up the silverware and napkins, touched the chairs, and made a comment about being able to sit down in a real chair to a real table inside a room. To anyone else, it was no big deal. To us it was. We had stood, sat on the ground, leaned against the bed of a pickup truck or trailer, sat on a rock, or just stood where there was room for almost two thousand miles and about one hundred twenty days. It was indeed a pleasure to sit down and be served. Years ago, when settlers came to a community after many miles and days on the trail, they would look around at sights in any community with total wonder on their faces. Those similarities between them and us were predominate again.

Time was ticking away; we were going to make it to the stockyards in Fort Worth. Nothing could stop the wheels of spirit. The public's opinion had begun to change. A wave of recognition had replaced a frown of doubt. I can't say people were not still apprehensive and saying we were still out of our minds. That was all right. We were clinging to every moment and every mile; the entire journey was almost a memory.

Chapter Seventy-two

The Texas Panhandle was beautiful, just as the rest of the state had been. Desert lands had a beauty, as did the mountains, or forests, or the hill country. As we rolled further into the panhandle, the small towns were out in force. The event had gained momentum and Texans were waiting for the train. Larger cities are caught up in a faster pace of living—traffic signs to tell them where a destination is or a colored light to tell them when to go or stop. We understood all of this and hoped the viewers of discontent felt just once as we passed by holding them up, only briefly, that this type of travel is what their forefathers went through to get them to that moment of frustration. After all, they still call the power under the hood of a car *horsepower* don't they?

Littlefield had crowds of welcomers. Mark Morton's mules broke away just as we came into camp. I had the misconception that they should have been tired. The speed they displayed out across the circle was not that of worn out animals.

Spring Lake was our next layover day. A huge cotton gin was camp. People came from Earth to welcome us and mingle with the pioneers. They passed out stickers wel-

coming us to Earth. That was probably the most appropriate greeting we had anywhere along the trail. Earth is a
town close to Spring Lake.

I had ridden along for a number of days watching the
lands pass by before us. There were fields of crops planted
for harvest later on and ranchers overseeing their herds of
stock. All of these things and more brought another poem
to mind that I put together just for people of that area:

A ranch house, a farmer,
A little child's hand,
The cactus or rivers
It's all Texas land.

Grass in a pasture,
Blue in the skys,
Spotted with clouds,
Through a pioneer's eyes.

Horses and cattle
Come running to us,
Then turn on their heels,
For they do not have trust.

Think of your ancestors.
Remember their battles,
When they gave up their birthlands
And took to their saddles.

Can't you see that light shining
From out of the past
Reaching toward us
And touching at last?

Just look at these wagons
That go down the road
Bringing to life
A story that's old.

Chapter Seventy-three

On toward Dimmit, Herford, and into Canyon, Texas, we were on our way to the northernmost point of our journey. Amarillo Canyon, just south of Amarillo, met us all with a change of weather. The camp was set up to serve dinner. There was a band to provide the music for our dance.

Vicky Hazzard's daughter came to the wagon train with visions of horrible things in mind. She had to leave her friends at home. There were no modern conveniences, plus she was not interested in riding a horse anywhere or sticking her feet into a pair of western boots. She had to be the one young lady that was turned completely around on the trip. She learned to ride a horse actually quite well, plus started wearing boots and not wanting to ever wear anything else. Ann is a pretty young lady and grew prettier inside because of the wagon train. She would create a dance if there was not one scheduled. Ann would miss another dance. After being served our meal, the winds hit Canyon. We all made hasty preparations to ready our campsites for the storm that hit us so suddenly. Frances Johnson, from Henrietta, Texas, was working on her wagon wheels. The wagon was propped up on supports. The wind blew that wagon over. I also heard two more wagons had blown over. There were no injuries, but it was frightening. Mother nature was going to give us hell. Dinner was cut short and the dance was cancelled. Extra ties were added to objects to keep the damage to a minimum. We were in Tornado Alley—not the most comforting thought. Local authorities usually kept us informed of coming bad weather throughout our trip. This saved us more times than I care to count.

Around ten that evening, I was settled in my quarters after moving Lady out of a corral up beside the camper to get her out of the wind. An urgent knock came at my door. I opened it to find Jan France standing in the rain. She called me to hold the door. Turning, she reached into her van and brought out two huge banana splits. We had started that habit back in Fort Hancock. This time, however, we would not have to fight the others. The wind rocked the camper and we sat eating our sinfully rich desserts, laughing like two children breaking the rules.

When the wagon train left Canyon, after a rough night with the weather, we were really in for a shock. The temperature was low. Most everyone had sent his or her long johns home to make more room in their quarters. I cannot say who was colder, the horseback riders or the teamsters. At least on a horse, the body heat from the animal was a help. At the same time, the icy winds could not be escaped no matter where one traveled. The rain continued throughout the entire day of travel. The teamsters fastened their canvases down to keep most of the foul weather out, but our wagons were not made like those of a century ago. The wagoneers helped one another out as best they could by loaning jackets, hats, gloves, or whatever was necessary to get us going. I remember Doyce Todd asking me if I had gloves as I rode by her into the storm. She and her husband Clyde traveled with us as our official tack supplier. I told her I would be all right but Miss Hazel would need a pair. She very kindly ran to the trailer/store and grabbed two pair of gloves and ran to catch me. Later,

I would realize how thoughtful she really was. Giving one pair to Miss Hazel we went off into our freezing day. The wagons rolled twenty-seven miles that day and we would forever remember every foot of that route. The cold would not stop. Freezing rain made my hands so cold even with the gloves. I felt for those travelers; there was no escape. We tipped our heads to the wind and rain and kept the animals moving. The horses and mules were not bothered in the least; they always walked out better in cool weather—in this case, cold weather.

Our lunch break was only long enough to water the stock and dash to the blue room. We were all more than willing to give up extra time in the miserable weather in order to get to camp. My hands froze to the reins and I knew I was not alone.

I glanced over my shoulder a time or two. The teamsters sat huddled, trying to stay as warm as possible. How the pioneers of a century ago ever did it was a mystery to me. They were luckier than we were in this case. They did not have a schedule to keep.

Arriving in camp north of Amarillo, we climbed down off our horses and out of our wagons to try to use limbs that did not cooperate. We were wet, frozen, and had to take care of the stock first. I would have given five dollars for a cup of hot chocolate.

No stalls or shelter for the horses were available. I tied Lady to a tree and went to catch the shuttle bus. Still in wet clothes, we were a sorry-looking lot. The rain did not let up when I tried to find my way back to the camp-grounds. My windshield wipers chose not to work and I missed the sign to turn. My wrong turn on the freeway system took me way off course. When I did finally find camp, the odometer read forty-nine miles and I knew we had only rolled twenty-seven. Asking for directions was a total joke. The first gentleman told me I was "way way" from the camp. I let him know I had traveled over two thousand miles to get there on a wagon train and asked, "Was it further than that?" Of course not, but he and I had a different view of what was long and what was not. I weaved my way around finally finding my way to the campgrounds. I parked under the tree at an angle to keep the wind off of my horse. She was shivering so bad I was quite worried. Two blankets later and an extra dose of oats with corn and she began to settle down. I rubbed her and tended to her until I was sure she was safe. Then it dawned on me how wet and cold *I* still was. Just then, Suzanne, Pam Blanscet, and Frances Johnson all came up and offered me a warm dry place for the night to stay in out of the cold. I accepted with one stipulation, I had to return to camp to check on Lady at five A.M. Mother nature was not going to win this round.

We all checked into a motel room and crashed after a hot shower. I made the run out to camp at five and the mare was in great shape. I fed her and returned to the room to continue my sleep.

Chapter Seventy-four

The Sesquicentennial Committee in Amarillo had gone to a lot of trouble, just as each community we had passed. They had wonderful entertainment and a campsite welcome we were all impressed with. Recognition and fanfare it was not necessary but it was fun.

During a welcoming ceremony our second day, we were treated to warm temperatures and many many vis-

itors. Charles Oliver asked me to share with the audience
the poem I had written for Amarillo:

We came into Amarillo
With the thunder and the rain,
Greeted by many thousands,
This Texas Wagon Train.

Mother nature was here waiting
With a chill throughout the air.
Our pioneers came rolling,
We wouldn't show that we did care.

From away toward east Texas
To the southlands of this state,
In from El Paso, Guadalupe,
Many many miles we'll make.

As progress came before us
From one hundred fifty years ago,
Our wagons are here showing
How that same progress had to go.

With guidance from the heavens,
Our people from across this land,
We're reaching out toward you.
We know you all do understand.

A three-day, three-night stay in Amarillo was used to
catch up, once again, with errands and chores. The institute
where we were staying went all out for the wagoneers:
hair care for the ladies, vehicle repairs, boots resoled—all
at no expense to the pioneers. A wonderful facility was

provided at our disposal. My boots had a big hole in each, so I rushed them over at the last minute to be repaired. The man in charge was very nice and helpful in allowing me to bring them at the last hour. I was able to make the rest of the journey without getting my feet wet every time I went to the water tanks to fill my buckets. We all benefited from Amarillo's thoughtfulness.

All the way around Texas, we were entertained by bands that were all special to us. Amarillo had the group "Mason Dixon" for our enjoyment. They played in the daylight hours when we were the most busy, so some of my traveling buddies and I walked over to the stage with curry combs, or hoof picks, or whatever tools we were using at the time to watch this fabulous group play some of their songs for us. They were worth the interruption to our chores.

Fred and Oma Cooper lived in Amarillo and had waited for us to get to their city. Both of them were retired and met the train often since we left Sulphur Springs to video the trip for museums at universities around Texas. They extended their most gracious hospitality to us. I took full advantage of their whirlpool. My leg was healing, but I was pushing too hard. The therapeutic effects were super.

Jan had her birthday the day we rolled out of Amarillo. A helicopter came to the campsite to pick her up and fly her over the train.

Claude, Texas, was our next stop; there were a few runaways the morning we pulled out of Amarillo. The stock had been rested well and were feeling extra good. Carol Crisp told me later how her incident with Boots happened. It seemed that Boots wanted to run all day instead of stay in line and walk like he was suppose to. Arriving in camp, the wagons were held up just briefly as the Winchester wagon was brought back into line after difficulty had caused Bill Tooley to lose his place in line.

Carol's husband was one of our assistant wagon masters and always traveled up and down the line of wagons. When the Winchester wagon passed Carol's little wagon, Gerald was leading. Boots was attached to his stable mate, Gerald's horse, and decided he was not to be left behind. Off Boots ran to catch up, narrowly missing a brick building but heading straight for a gas meter in the yard. Carol was pulling and tugging for all she was worth. Again Boots got by another obstruction and raced on toward a trailer house down a deep gulley. Perry Jo Frost raced to stop the runaway. Perry Jo should have been a stunt man; he was probably one of the best hands we had on the trail. Carol was shook but uninjured. I think she renamed Boots, but I can't print it. Coming into Clarandon after being hosted by Claude and Ashtola, we were approaching the "Hands Across America" weekend. Fred Shivers was to have a birthday, so the Vet and I did a little decorating. He sprayed my hand with white oil base paint and I put handprints all over Fred's big wheel horse, Ranger. Fred tried to find the prankster who marked his horse. When I told him it was me, my confession was met with lots of laughter instead of scorn. Neither Fred nor Debbie believed me. Pam Blanscet was standing close by and she was the main suspect. Poor Pam, she couldn't convince them she was innocent, and I couldn't convince them I was guilty.

A watering trough was dedicated in the town square as we brought the wagons down tree-lined streets with old trees touching their limbs above our heads. The wagon master dismounted and led his horse to be watered in the trough. I led Lady too, but the closeness of the crowd with their cameras clicking away made her nervous. This, the old saying: "You can lead a horse to water . . . " was most true at that point.

Carol and Gerald Crisp had another episode with Boots after we came into camp. Gerald unhitched Boots from one wagon and hitched him up to the new wagon the Crisps had just brought. The "new" wagon was one hundred and eleven years old. They had purchased the wagon from a seller in the last camp in Ashtola. The wagon was to be driven to Matt Williams' camp to have the wheel shrunk. Again, good 'ole Boots startèd looking for his stable mate. The new wagon was much heavier and made different noises than what Boots was accustomed to. Boots spooked. Gerald took two wraps around his hands with the lines and still could not slow Boots down. Boots went straight for a pickup, and almost missed it, but caught the front fender. Gerald was jerked out of the wagon onto the ground and dragged a ways before he could get his hands unwrapped and released. Boots ran faster. The shafts were pulled out and the single tree slapped up against Boots' legs and he went crazy with fright. Boots was almost back to his own camp when a vehicle came into view. He hit that fender also and continued on his way to his camp. The new wagon Gerald and Carol bought was sent home to be repaired. Boots was uninjured.

Chapter Seventy-five

Jo Ann Theilemann had started the train ride with a bucksin mare that was in foal. During the night, in Bryce, the foal was born, and what a beauty she was!

This was the first stop we had made that one of the community members asked me to write a poem for their area. Bryce, Texas, is an intersection. However, there must be a large populated area somewhere. Every place we looked hundreds of visitors walked around our camp. They enjoyed their poem:

> Plowed fields along a roadway,
> Wheat crops are flowing.
> The wagon train is passing
> While the North Red River is rolling.
>
> A rancher brands his cattle
> With his wife near by his side.
> He looks out across his homeland,
> Holding his ancestors pride.
>
> The feelings from last century
> Come before us on this day.
> We wouldn't trade our feelings
> Or stop those smiles along the way.
>
> When Autumn comes this year
> And harvests have been sowed,
> Take time to thank the maker
> Plus the wonders of the old.
>
> We have come out here before you
> To show the times of all our pasts.
> You've reached silently toward us
> And our memories will last.

The pioneers of the eighties would always remember the piney wood trees in east Texas and other sights along the way. Both from nature and man, seeing the Red River up close was to be another unforgettable sight as we rolled on toward Turkey, Texas. The hills came abruptly and the teams earned their oats that day. I had always heard of the Red River sand and how truly red it was, but I was not prepared for the splendor of the red and the beautiful countryside that surrounded us all day long.

We traveled down into small canyons and up to the heights of peaks that most of us did not know were even there.

I was in the Shivers wagon that day. We were almost out of the hills when Fred noticed the WBAP wagon took off suddenly down the bar ditch. Glyn had his team under control quickly. Fred was saying he thought WBAP was having a problem when he looked down without changing his tone and added, "Fred is having trouble also." Just then, his five-up hitch decided to take a right turn and march right up to the fence line across the bar ditch. It is a startling sensation to look down and have the entire team disappear in one step. No damage—George Fletcher and Paul Lawrence quickly had the team back on the road.

Turkey, Texas is the home of the very famous country swing band leader, Bob Wills. We were to stay in Turkey for two nights and we loved it. Word had spread that we would have turkey dinner with all the trimmings. What a treat—with all the homemade goodies! Turkey was about to witness how a wagoneer can stack a plate with food higher than anyone on Earth.

When I called Bobby later, we were talking about a bad storm that had hit Forth Worth. Before I hung up, the police came and told us we were in for a serious rain storm also. The lightning was striking everywhere. Quentin came and told me I would have to evacuate my camp spot; it was in the line of the flood waters they were sure would hit some time during the night. I had not parked near the wagons throughout the journey before, until Turkey. Moving everything in the wind, lightning, and rain, plus the dark, is not fun. Therefore, I learned: stick to the usual plan when it came to parking.

The rains came. We tried to have everything covered

up. The stock had to wait this one out. We did have plenty
of huge trees to help shelter them. It still felt like a garden
hose had been turned on us.

Sunday morning we came out of our wet campground
to attend church services that were to be held outside. I
shared the poem I had put together for Turkey:

> Covered wagons moving,
> Red River sands,
> God's country greet us
> In this northern land.
>
> People on the hilltops,
> Teams struggled with the roads,
> Wildlife stood watching
> All the teamsters and their loads.
>
> Pioneers remembering,
> Reaching back in time,
> Uncles, aunts, and grandparents
> Built this land so fine.
>
> Wagons out here circled
> Beneath those mighty trees,
> Sheltered from the rain storm,
> Protected by the leaves.
>
> This tiny town in Texas
> Welcomed us so strong
> Like those that came before us
> Back when Bob Wills sang his song.

After the services were completed, we walked over
to the hall for our turkey dinner. I can testify; we stuffed

ourselves beyond belief. The ladies of the town had outdone themselves; the food was not just good, it was excellent. We spent the rest of the day lying around and trying to move normally again. Some of the wagoneers set up a card table on the sidewalk in front of the bank. It was quite a picture to see these people dressed in their pioneer clothing playing table games and being photographed by fascinated onlookers.

Rains threatened us again, not too many went far from camp.

Fred and Oma Cooper were with us again. Fred had just passed the Cooper Ranch on to the next Cooper generation. It was located seven miles southwest of town. He and his aunt were old-timers of the community.

The next morning, we had to pass through a deep mudhole. The teams met another challenge. I cannot praise the animals enough. They never failed to do whatever was necessary to get the wagons down the road. The teamsters had come a long ways. We were all stronger in many ways. We had to keep the wagons moving fast; the mudhole grew deeper. The big wagons were safe, but the small wagons, Luns, Nelson, smaller wagons with smaller teams had to really pull. We made for an exciting exit out of town with mud flying, teamsters hollering, and outriders whooping.

Passing through the small town of Matador and on to the open camp at Glenn, Texas, we were getting close enough to the end of our journey to pick up a lot more wagons and riders. Plus, we were approaching some big ranches that were to hosts the wagon train. For those of us that had come the whole day, we had looked forward to these big ranches with great anticipation.

The days of knowing who everyone was in camp had passed. When the participants arose, they found the camp had grown during the night, and new faces met all of them at dawn. In a way, we would miss the closeness of the core of the wagon train since we had all stuck together throughout the hardships and walked step by step together in brotherhood.

Some of our new arrivals had been with us at a prior date but had returned to their homes for valid reasons. We all welcomed their return and always asked if they could stay until the end.

As the wagon train arrived in a small town that not many of us had ever heard of, called Dickens, we were welcomed by a lonely rider off to our right as we made the left turn down a slight incline toward town. What a beautiful sight to see that grey horse with its rider sitting atop a tall pile of boulders, greeting the pioneers from the past. We couldn't help but think that a wagon train last century must have been met like that so long ago.

After a brief stop around the courthouse for a welcoming ceremony, we continued on to camp.

Pam Blanscet and I went down to where the horses she was in charge of were tied. We had to doctor two of them. Then we took all five up the hill to where we were camped. She sat on the back door area of my camper and held the lines to all five. We did not give a thought about doing such a thing. However, Pam told me later we could not have attracted more attention if we would have led them to camp in the nude. I preferred driving.

We left Dickens at seven the next morning, traveling just a few miles on the highway, then turning to enter to the Pitchfork Ranch. Some of the ranch hands stood at the gate to welcome us personally as we passed through. Younger hands were all excited about our arrival and just the general excitement that was always stirred by our arrival. Older hands looked at us with different appreciation.

I rode Pam's horse, Bo, that day. Bo did not always pay attention to things. After passing through the gates, Bo took a different route than everyone else which resulted in him stepping into a cluster of cactus. George Fletcher rode up and dismounted to remove the quills from both hind feet. Mr. Fletcher took his time and had Bo ready to go before long. I thanked him and turned just in time to see five wagons get in trouble at the same time. The first wagon hit the lip on the dirt roadway we were on and snapped the tongue off sending the wagon into the air, dumping both wagoneers on the ground. The team spooked and ran off, still connected by their traces. The second wagon, driven by John and Mary Bess Edwards, hit the fenceline. The tongue was snapped off by the impact on the fence. Another team was racing away in fright. The next wagon was pulled off out through the brush with Perry Jo in hot pursuit to catch them. John Edwards had been jerked out of his wagon. I raced up to each group of teamsters to see if medical help was needed. Two more teams were racing away in another direction. Mike Lowery was catching loose teams as were others that could help and not get in the way. How injury was avoided, I don't know. But everyone was safe. Trailers were sent to get the broken wagons on to camp and we continued on our way.

Before an hour passed after the runaway, I faced a test that I had given plenty of thought to but had hoped would never come about. I heard a rattler to my left, just as I urged Bo up off of the dirt road into the brush. We could not all travel on the road at once because it was to narrow. Therefore, in places, the riders would step up out of the way. I didn't even look down, I stuck the spurs to him but he had to kick at the snake first. Not a safe idea. Just as Bo kicked, the snake struck. His leg was too high and the snake was too low with its strike. I really stuck the spurs then. Ezra Gingerich jumped from his horse and killed the snake, as he held the rattler up for all to see, Bo reared, whirled, and ran. I had to laugh; his timing was great.

Lunch was out by old catch pens that must have been there for many many years. A beautiful setting.

As soon as we rolled again, we were in steep hills. It started to rain which made the dirt passageway slippery. WBAP had problems with their wagon but with the aid of a saddle horse pulling a rope from the tongue on the wagon, they made it up without further delay. Boyd Ivey had a six-up hitch but seven more horsepower were needed to help him up also. Miss Hazel's wagon had a problem with one of the team. The driver did not know how to drive and had the limping mule pulling most of the load. The driver refused help. This was not unusual for new drivers; they did not know when help was really in their best interest.

We weaved our way down off of the hill into camp. Not everyone came into camp at once. The rain hampered our progress, and the rain was split up in several places. Just as the first wagon started the circle in camp, a young man ran to meet us with the carcass of a five and one-half foot rattler. We were warned to be cautious. The last wagon came into camp more than an hour behind the first, but something was wrong; Boyd Ivey had not made it. After all the trouble he had just getting over the hills, he had broken an axle a half mile out from camp. We could see him up the roadway. Help was sent to him and we all watched as the time passed on. The repairs were made and he was towed by a tractor into camp just before it turned dark. He told me later that was all he wanted, to be in camp before it was dark.

The Pitchfork Ranch made their branding iron available for the wagoneers so we could put their mark on our gear or wagons as the other ranches had allowed us to do. The truck was set up in the circle of wagons to do the branding. Most of us carried what we wanted branded over to the branding area. Throughout the wagons, one could walk down the line of the circle and see the spring seats or sides of each and see various brands we had had along the trail. Debbie Shivers had Kay Lightfoot help her carry their spring seat to the fire to be branded. I had just finished having my chaps done and had turned to speak to the photographer, Doug, when I heard my name called from somewhere behind me, but I really didn't pay attention. Then I heard my name called in desperation. Turning, I saw a look of total shock on Debbie's face. A rattler was crawling over her foot. I turned slowly, not wanting to panic anyone with sudden movement. Seeing the snake, I called to the fellas around the branding fire, "Guys, guys, guys! There's a rattler!" Absolutely no response came from them. I called once more. They turned slowly and one of them mumbled something about what all the trouble was. I called out again; "rattler!" and pointed to Debbie, still frozen to her spot with the snake laying across her boot. The men, tough frontiersmen that they were, turned back to their branding. I ran to the back of a pickup nearby, grabbed a shovel and ran back to the woman. Just then, a blonde woman reached down and chopped off the head of the snake as Kay Lightfoot held it with a stick. The head was snapping, so I kicked it over into a shallow hole and shoveled dirt on top of it. I could not resist calling back to the men around the fire: "It's all right guys, the girls did fine without your assistance! Don't interrupt yourselves!" I guess the ruggedness of the pioneer women had just caught up with us. Men were not always available.

Helen Jones, her daughter Tooter, and grandchildren

Kit and Stephen rejoined us on the Pitchfork. It was really good to see them again and have them back on the train. I ate dinner at their camp that night and caught up on all that had been going on with them during their absence. Hogg had not returned with Helen due to prior commitments. Tooter would have to assist her mother, but I knew those two ladies would do just fine without much help from another.

Another big talent show had been planned for the layover, as we would be on the ranch for two nights. New talent was beginning to come forward. Mr. Macey Nelson of Alpha, Illinois, our usual Suzanne Whitfield, J. W. Jines with his harmonica, and even Teresa Shivers and Pam Blanscet did a very funny rendition of a dance created to entertain children, but had all of us rolling on the ground with laughter. Helen Jones sang us a very touching song she had written for us. One of the McCrosson boys, Jerry, had asked me to write him a poem because he was going home in three more days. I wrote it and dedicated it to all of the boys from the boys' ranch. I asked them to come to the talent show together where I shared it with all of them:

> From Sioux Falls, South Dakota,
> To the south lands of this state,
> It's a long way from your homeland,
> But you helped us celebrate.
>
> Big Belgians in the harness,
> Flags a flying high,
> Trucks to help you travel,
> We're friends now, you and I.
>
> Remember all you've learned
> Along this road of cheers;

Always hold your head up,
Keep the memories, through the years.

Think back and have some pride
In all you've done and seen.
Walk into life a winner
Standing tall and wearing green.

Take time to thank the master
For the sun and also rain,
And always do remember
The Texas Wagon Train.

The McCrosson Boys' Ranch was made up of young boys from the age of twelve to sixteen. They had been sent to the boys' ranch with disciplinary problems or other reasons such as problems in their homes.

It was my observation that each one of the boys that came to the wagon train each time they were rotated, knew very little about horses. They each had their daily animal to care for. I further observed they would come to camp with ideas far different than what they learned along the trail. They always wore their uniform shirts of green and set up their camp just a bit away from the rest of the wagoneers. The McCrosson Boys' Ranch was also a sponsor of the wagon train. The ranch is the home of the Shaffer Belgian Horse farm in Sioux Falls, South Dakota.

This wagoneer had admiration for those young men and will always remember how they helped Texas take another step into history in the true Old West fashion. They had received these words with appreciation, and I was proud of all those young men.

I waited another hour to do an additional piece I had written especially for the ranch. I wanted to give the poem

to the manager of the ranch, but he was at another part
of the spread and couldn't make it back. Later, he received
a copy and sent word of appreciation. He informed me
that the piece would go up in the headquarters of the ranch:

> An old rancher stood there watching
> As the covered wagons pass,
> Remembering his father's words
> Somewhere out of the past
>
> About the branding of the cattle,
> Fence lines stretched across the ranch,
> Windmills turning slowly,
> And how a cowboy took a chance.
>
> They called the spread the Pitchfork
> When land was vast you see
> Around a hundred years ago,
> Back in eighteen eighty-three.
>
> Quarter horses, cattle,
> Acres of red land,
> Open up the gates,
> The wagons crossed the dirt and sand
>
> He may recall the days
> When the wagons brought the settlers,
> Shared life and work and dreams
> And made the best kind of neighbors.
>
> Erase the years of time.
> Let a century go by.
> An old rancher stands there watching,
> A wagon train has caught his eye.

Bobby came to camp a little after midnight that night. I had not seen him for thirty-two days and was very excited to have him with me for a few days. (I hoped anyway. I would never ask him when he had to return home).

The rains accompanied us out of camp on toward the 6666 Ranch. We made a lunch stop in Guthrie. Everyone in the county must have shown up in that tiny town to see the train. There was music, games, an art show, and plenty of food to eat.

When Garry called "wagons ho!" to bring the wagons out of Guthrie and on to camp, Rudi Nelson was not in his usual driver's seat on the stagecoach. Mark Morton and Fred Shivers climbed aboard and took the lines to the six-up hitch. Rudi caught up with the train about a mile down the road. We all let him have it with a lot of teasing. His good nature brought him through, but red-faced. Wagoneers held nothing back when it came to ribbing one another.

Bobby had moved the camper up for me, and I had more time for fun things instead of catching the shuttle bus back to camp. After we returned from town to restock supplies, we came around the corner of the roadway to see our camper anchored to the ground with six ropes. I laughed and laughed. Jan and Garry were parked right next to us and I knew they had been the guilty parties. I got out and called to Jan. With the utmost innocence she said, "Oh, hello." She did not admit to anything until I asked just who knew about this anchoring. Again an innocent tone, "Why, only the Four Six outfit camped just over the fenceline from us. They furnished all of the material." Great. Now everyone knew. It was always a good time to bring to life the visits of spouses on these occasions. Bobby and I had not escaped. After all the laughter settled down, we got on with the chores. The Four Six outfit had been traveling with us for a few days. They would set up their camp with huge tents to cook and sleep under for a large number of people. Bobby was sitting in one of the lawn chairs just outside our door to the camper when four attractive ladies from the Four Six approached the fence that separated their camp from ours. We had not met them prior to that moment but one of them looked my husband right in the eye and asked, "Sir, are you the gentleman that has been gone for thirty-two days?" I almost fell out of the camper laughing. Bobby looked most uncomfortable, and said, "Yes, ma'am."

At the entrance to the Spike Box Ranch in Benjamin, a very special monument had been made to honor the wagon train. It would be left there permanently. The forthought had been activated long before our arrival and was a warming thought.

We were still being plagued by the rains. On the trail, the rain kept us cooler, but the campsites were turned into nightmares.

Visitors for all of us began to visit us regularly. This would be the rule most of the way on into Fort Worth. We were nearing the end of the trial and visitors were beginning to build up momentum along with us. My very special friend from Arlington, Texas met the train in Benjamin. Pam had not had the opportunity to see the wagons roll, so her visit was special for both of us.

Many activities were planned for us. Most of them turned out but the rain got the dance again.

Our flu epidemic had died out, oddly enough our colds had disappeared too. We were always in the rain and wet most of the time, but stronger I guess, to help ward off most of the maladys we had encountered along the trail.

While on the Spike Box ranch, David Shivers had his

birthday. Early on the second morning of our stay, Pam Blanscet, James Simmons, Frances Johnson, Scott (Mr. Simmons grandson) and I decorated David's wagon in the only manner we could think of. We borrowed all the toilet paper we could from everywhere and wrapped it all around his wagon. Right in the middle of the operation, Pam stopped suddenly and ask James Simmons if he thought we would corrupt his grandson by having him around us while we pulled off our tricks. I couldn't help but laugh out loud in what was to be our quiet setting. I told her with a grandfather like James Simmons, there wasn't anything we were going to do to damage the lad. The night before David had gone to sleep with eight head of Percheron bay horses, and awoke to eight head of sorrel mules. He promptly got us back within the hour by turning them all loose at once. What a mess that was. That was not the end however. Pam and I went to get one of the Percherons, "Belle," and I painted her with congratulatory words for David, in bright orange paint. Mike Jackson, from Truscott, Texas was watching the entire episode; I asked him when his birthday was; he assured me there was absolutely no way he was ever going to tell me when it was. He stood by that until the end of the trail, too. I don't know why.

Chapter Seventy-six

The first wedding on the wagon train was to be in Abilene. Mike Lowery would make his lady Shawna, Mrs. Lowery. Planning a wedding on the trail was no easy matter with constant moving and details to be worked out. It was with the cooperation of the city of Abilene that the occasion was made special. Ray Bosehart and his wife Aleen had been traveling with us for a long time; they had been very instrumental in preparing the committee for our stay in their town. The wedding took place in the Ray Bosehart Arena on the campgrounds.

Chapter Seventy-seven

Just outside of Abilene, between Haskell and Stamford, I rode with Helen Jones's and Jimmy Daniels's wagons. It had reached the point where floating between two wagons was more enjoyable. One could visit back and forth with both drivers and pass the long miles away in no time.

Helen Jones walked out to her wagon every single morning in a colorful frontier dress and matching bonnet. She always had her makeup on and looked a wonderful part of the wagon train. I will admit that the rest of us girls going down the road gave up makeup and fashions for a more comfortable look. However, I commend Helen for her never ending efforts that brought a shining light to our train with her smile and attitude.

The camp in Stamford was a parking lot near the activity building on the fair grounds. Logs and dips were in the parking lot. We were to ride down existing rows to circle the wagons. Helen pulled her wagon up and stopped just behind Jimmy Daniel's. The wagons were to be circled in a double row to get them all inside the area. Other wagons were passing to the left of Helen's team; she was out of the wagon holding the team. Tooter and I dismounted; Jimmy and Mike were at the head of their teams too. A loud sudden noise made Helen's team nervous. I stepped up and grabbed the left team horse. Helen was standing between the team, calming the animals. Another wagon passed making a louder noise as they crossed the dip. The horse I was holding reared straight up, jerking the leadline out of my hand and lounging over against Helen. I grabbed her arm and jerked her out of the way. Tooter screamed to her two kids in the wagon to jump. Kit came out. Stephen clung to the springseat. The horses were off like lightning with Stephen hanging onto the seat. Tooter yelled again for Stephen to jump. Everything happened so quickly, no one could grab the boy. Tooter raced off on foot after the runaway wagon. Somehow she caught that wagon and grabbed Stephen out of the seat. If I would not have seen it, I would not have believed it. The frightened team ran on. To the end of the parking lot they went. Turning quickly to the left, they pulled a small tree out of the ground as the wagon passed over it. Along the fenceline they raced; tree limbs flew everywhere. Running in such a panic, they had become dangerously wild. Garry and Perry Jo came on a run to help. Tooter ran toward the team, not thinking about the act; she just wanted them to stop so no one else would be hurt. The wild team had made a full circle and were running toward the rest of the wagon circle. It appeared that they could not be stopped and another wagon, unaware, was in serious danger. Charles Welch saw what was coming. He put his huge team of Shires in the pathway of the runaways; they had to be stopped. We all froze; it was going to be a horrible wreck. The frightened team was three strides from the Welch wagon when they suddenly dropped to the ground as if shot. The wagon turned over on its side and came apart. The logs in the parking lot had a lot of grass around them. The runaway team had stepped on one, tripped them and brought the whole mess to a standstill immediately. The team had fallen at the feet of Charlie's team. Tooter became hysterical over Stephen's close call; her horse had been tied to the wagon when the runaway started. Garry grabbed her to calm her down. I was trying to find her horse. I truly could not remember what the animal looked like. Tooter started to run frantically calling the horse. I saw someone leading a horse toward us and called out to Tooter to see if it was the right one. I had my hand on her arm. She jerked it away telling me right quick, "That was not her mount." I just said, "All right, maybe this one over here." She was so upset she did not realize what she had done, and we laughed about that moment later. Finally, another rider came up on her horse and the poor woman totally collapsed with emotion. The men from the train got together and reassembled Helen's wagon. They refused pay and had her ready to roll out of camp with us the next morning. Many late night hours had been spent to do the kindness.

The wagon train was scheduled to stop in Anson, but was changed to Hawley because of the mud. Even that plan got us all into a mudhole.

I rode in the Shivers's wagon that day. Pam Blanscet and I both helped Fred drive to relieve him for much needed rest. The rains had left behind humidity; that was an enemy to the working horses and mules. Pam and I noticed Ranger was getting overheated as was Star. We called back to get Fred up and have him take a look at the horses. Without stopping the team, Fred jumped down and looked at the team closely to see if they should be pulled or left in the hitch and go on into camp. There were deep water holes alongside the road. Fred thought if he could get some of the water and pour it on the overheated horses, they may make it on to camp. The practice was not thought of favorably when we first started to have trouble with the teams overheating and there are many who may think it won't work now, but it became a common practice on the wagon train and it always worked. Fred grabbed one of the buckets out from under the wagon after asking me if I thought I could hold all five horses when he hit them with the water. I said I could, with total recall of these powerful animals running away over in East Texas. Fred ran to get the water, then came back alongside the horses and tossed it. Ranger jerked up and over, ramming into Tex, and Belle did about the same with Star, but I knew it was coming and taking a double wrap with the lines I held them. The whole routine was repeated and we made it on into camp.

Later in camp, Pam was waiting anxiously for her fella to come and see her. The opportunity could not be passed. She had had an accident with one of the big draft horses stepping on her a few days earlier and had to resort to using crutches. Fred Shivers offered to help her get over to the blue room, and of course after that she was on her own. I was helping Frances Johnson and David Shivers at the time care for all the horses they had put together because of Pam's injury—twenty-one head. I came upon the scene with Pam in the blue room a short while later. She had been locked in the unit by Fred and was screaming for release. Fred hollered at me that I could do whatever I wanted to help her be more comfortable, but I couldn't let her out. James Simmons had brought her reading materials. Word had been received that her fella was on the premises and we wanted to be sure and find her. She made so much noise, I think everyone in Abilene knew where she was. She was only in the outhouse an hour and a half; just how much suffering can one go through in that length of time?

The rain had turned our camp to mud. The support vehicles were stuck, the trailers were stuck, and wagoneers were spread out for over four miles in every direction you could see.

Chapter Seventy-eight

I was on a countdown. Donya had written to me that my first grandchild would be making an appearance around the twentieth of this month, June. I wrote my daughter to tell her as soon as the baby was born to call the state troopers and let them bring the message. They always had to bring bad news; this time they could smile upon delivery! Then Bobby and I had spoken by phone, and we put our heads together. My daughter was to have a midwife tend her at the birth so why not have the baby on the wagon train. I thought it was a great idea, but I was not giving birth. We would see. Helen Jones and I had discussed it too; we had just the wagon picked out for the occasion.

Rolling into Abilene, we made preparations for our two-day stay. The sun had come out and started to dry things off. We were met by a sad occurrence. Cash, Mike Lowery's trick roping horse, was seriously ill. Mike and Shawna's wedding was the next day and this was not going to help the festivities. The vets worked on Cash day and night the entire stay; it was sad to see the animal that had come so far struggle hard just to cling to life.

I had my camp set up close to Pam's as we had taken to doing almost daily. Bobby was coming to get me and return to Fort Worth; our sixteen-year–old grandson had qualified for the North Texas High School Rodeo Finals and I wanted to be there to cheer him on. Cory had worked hard to achieve his top placing going into the finals.

The facility around our camp was a perfect accommodation for horses. The 4-H had a show going on at the same time as our arrival so we were not allowed to use the corrals, but the bathhouse for the horses was perfect. I, along with many other wagoneers, took our horses inside to wash a lot of trail dirt out of their hides. Lady loved it.

She had been accustomed to baths throughout the years I had had her until now. Bobby pulled up just as I was leading the mare back to camp. Frances had said she would care for Lady in my absence. I was only going to be gone overnight. The wedding was the next day and I did not want to miss it.

We secured the mare in my camp and I hollered out to Frances I was going. Bobby wanted to stop and tell Jan and Garry something, I had no idea what. I was anxious to get started. As soon as we walked in the France house, Bobby excused himself. Jan and Garry had a house full of visitors. Jan asked me what Bobby was doing. I told her one never knew about him. He then returned to the camper with a bottle of champagne. My first thought was of how good Cory must have done as he had ridden the night before also. Bobby handed the bottle to me to open while he passed around glasses. Then he said Cory had been bucked off the first go around. I wanted to know if he was hurt. Now I was confused. He then added that he had missed the performance the night before. I knew immediately what it was. My grandchild had been born! I yelled and screamed and jumped up and down! There was no way to calm me. I was so excited! Jan grabbed me and so did Garry. I continued to jump around. I ran outside and told everyone I could see, "I'm a grandmother, it's a boy!" I ran and ran. Everyone was applauding and laughing. I told strangers. I hugged people. I told the whole world. I had never been so excited over anything. I do not know if becoming a grandparent affected others this way, but it sure did me. I will never forget the next thing Bobby told me. He had talked it over with Donya; she had agreed it would be a good thing to have the baby on the wagon train. She was packed and ready to come. Preston Robert Caulder Anthony Salles had decided otherwise. His initials are P.R.C.A. Now that's a way to keep the west alive.

We left camp to return to Fort Worth, my formal introduction to my grandson was coming. He had been born in my house with the capable assistance of a midwife. I joked with my husband how the women of his household had turned the clock back a hundred years this year. He sat in the room adjacent to the room where the baby was born the whole seventeen hours of labor. He just did survive the ordeal.

I returned to Abilene the next day but missed the wedding. My grandson had taken more time which was all right. I did hear that the ceremonies were started by Garry calling "wagons ho!" and leading the procession into the Ray Bosehart Indoor Arena. Ray drove the bride inside in a surry. Most of the guests came in their nicest frontier clothes. The preacher rode in on a mule and the entire affair was like a ceremony straight out of the 1800s. At the closing, Mike picked up his rope that he had entertained so many with along the trail and built a huge coil. He twirled it around his and his bride's heads. This is called a wedding ring. It fell down around them as he grabbed her and planted the traditional kiss. The photos I saw later were fabulous. The cowboy and his lady stepped into the surry and started their life together.

Chapter Seventy-nine

The lunch stop in Albany, Texas found us circled in front of an old folks home. I dismounted and walked over to where the group was waiting for us. They were all most anxious to see the wagoneers. Others followed me and we stopped by each person to ask what they thought, and thanked them for being there for us. Some of them hung onto us and just did not let go. With them, we just took more time. They usually just wanted to say something more about when they had come to the area many years earlier in a covered wagon and felt so appreciative. We understood. Unlike us, the oldest members of these homes had more authentic tales to tell than we ever would.

Chapter Eighty

Fort Griffin was a duplication of our last night in Abilene when we were warned of a coming storm and had to put all of the livestock inside. However, Fort Griffin had no covered shelter. I had parked under a big tree. Lady was tied close with blankets on to protect her from the hail that was reported on its way, too. The rains came in torrents. The tree helped, but everything was soaked. With the warning we had, there was not enough time to get things put away before we were hit.

We were still traveling north; the end of the trail was not far off. Throckmorton, then Olney, Archer City, they were all waiting and so were we. In Olney, after a warm dinner, we were in the usual muddy field. This was getting old. Doug Kafka had a horse get down under his horse trailer and get cut up seriously. I jumped in the truck with him to go get the vet. We were camped all over town and I only thought I knew where he was. The horse was in trouble and needed immediate help. We found Doctor Ken right outside of the main gate.

Afterwards, I wandered around camp to visit with my friends. I had not had the time to spend with them as I seemed to before. Apache and Vickie Barrett, Albert and Alice Nicely, Travis and Alene Reeves, Glen Worley, Betty McGahea, and J. R. Newton, the McCrosson boys, J. W. And Dort Jines, Mr. and Mrs. Bagwell, I wanted to see all of those wonderful people and more, but there wasn't time. We were coming home.

Chapter Eighty-one

Windthorst was muddy when we pulled in. Some of the teams struggled to get the wagons into camp. Some bogged down and had to be unhitched and the tractor brought out to get the wagons unstuck. The town was out in force to welcome us to their pretty little town, but the weather was out of any mortal's hands as we were about to find out.

The usual activities took place in camp plus games had been put together for our participation and enjoyment. The wagoneers had developed muscles that they didn't get to use too often—not with an audience. My favorite was the tug of war between the young high school boys and our McCrosson boys. Both teams were equal in age. Windthorst had their team of guys dig in and prepare for the competition. The McCrossons, coaxed by their chaperons, sat in their designated spots to start the game. I mentioned to the lady seated next to me on a bale of hay placed for onlookers, that I did not know what the town's folk did for daily exercise, but I did know what the McCrosson bunch did. Then I added that it would only take seconds for the Boys' Ranch to pull that rope over the line. I spoke a lot more sure of myself than I should have. However it took the McCrossons less than a minute to win. I glanced over and decided to leave my bale of hay.

Bobby and my daughter drove in at ten with the new baby. I was very happy to see them but we had just been warned about a serious storm. My daughter, Donya, had just settled in the overhead bunk of the camper when Paul Lawrence threw open the door and yelled for us to hang on. We had to get out of the field fast. The rains had hit and every available vehicle that could get out had to move immediately or wait for a tractor. Bobby jumped in the other truck and we were off like the wind. Donya cradled the baby as I clung to whatever I could to stand up. The camper rocked back and forth, swaying as if it might tip over. I glanced out the window to see a horrible sight; we were dangerously close to other cars and campers trying to get out of the mud too. The rain was coming down in torrents. I just crossed my fingers and prayed that Paul could get us out in an upright position. We slowed down once as another truck went in front of us. I heard the engine racing and felt the tires slip. We were stuck and would not make it. Paul kept working the truck and we came out of the mud as quick as we went in. I checked out the window again. If we could make fifty more yards we would be free. The only light came from the headlights. The rain was blinding and I did not know where Bobby was in all the confusion. The truck made one last dip and we were up out of the muddy field. Donya was still in the overhead bunk. I was on the floor, the only place I could find where I would not fall. My husband had not made it out, but flagging down one of the tractors got him out and able to join us shortly.

I grabbed my rainslick and jumped out into the storm to check the horses. They had been tied to the fenceline alongside the camper. I wanted to make sure Lady was secured to the fence as the thunder and lightning would go on all night long. She was frightened by the confusion and needed to be calmed. My idea to keep her tied to the fence was not bad, as she was out of the way. But I had overlooked one thing. She was tied in the ditch area with the other horses and come morning, they stood in about two and a half feet of water. It was funny, but only later.

The next morning, camp was broke and we all moved out at different times. The wagons took over an hour leaving. Teams pulled again with the necessary strength to get those wagons on their way. But that night in Windthorst would never be forgotten as a total disaster in camp. It was unfortunate that we do not remember the wonderful people that greeted us so warmly and hosted us so well. Only that damn rain storm!

Chapter Eighty-two

Wichita Falls camp at Sikes Senter Shopping Mall was an unusual place to put a wagon train, but it worked out all right. The mud was there in abundance. We did have an area available to us on the parking lot surface also. Standing livestock on pavement for two days is not a good thing to do. We had a grassy area, but not all of it could be used as part of it was under a foot of water.

Eight miles from camp, Bobby and Donya took me out to catch the train. As my daughter and I stood there watching the lead wagon, Bobby took my grandson and started off down the highway with him. He held him close enough but quickly caught the front wagon and handed that seven-day–old baby up to Jan's waiting hands. Preston slept through the entire transfer and even on into camp. I caught the Morrison Mills wagon and watched out the back, waving and greeting the crowds of welcomers as we passed over the city limits sign on into Wichita Falls. I thought about the baby, as he was so young and without his mother to comfort him, I didn't know what Jan would do if he awakened. Cindy Langford had been with the wagon train for a few days with her husband Rickey, and had caught the wagon with me just out of camp. Passing Donya and Bobby waving to us alongside the roadway, they had followed to check and see that the baby was all right. Circling the wagons at Sikes Senter, I walked up to get my grandson from Jan. We were overrun with people asking about this week old baby that had become a member of the Texas Wagon Train. It seems the news media had picked up on the little guy in the front wagon and he had made quite a splash for such a tiny bundle. I made my way to our campsite with Preston in my arms, answering all the questions and posing for pictures. I handed him back to his mother and the very first thing she said to him was, "Did you get your share of the residuals?" Stage mothers!

Charles Oliver asked the baby's full name and had him honored at the ceremonies that night. Preston was awarded with a handmade quilt donated by the employees of the K-Mart on the Loop in Wichita Falls. Each square was made to represent a symbol of Texas history, hand-stitched with the maker's name.

Chapter Eighty-three

Pam Blanscet, Randy Chadwick, Betty McGahea, Tooter Smith, Frances and Debbie Johnson, were all from Henrietta, Texas, our next stop. Pam had invited about fifty of the wagoneers to her house in Henrietta, as her mother was planning a large feast for us and a nice welcome to their town. Pam rode to the front of the train with Garry and Vern Renz to lead us into her town. This was always such a proud thing for any of the participants to do. Her relatives had made welcome home signs and were out in force to greet the lady that had walked around Texas with pride and honor. In the town square, we passed another sign from the city, welcoming all of their citizens back home that had participated.

My brother-in-law, sister-in-law, mother-in-law, aunts, and many more of my relatives came to visit us in Henrietta. I shared stories with them and we all feasted on a great meal provided by the community. I did make it over to Pam's house to put in an appearance and be polite. But Fay Blanscet was so gracious to me, I ended up staying the night. She had outdone herself with the food preparations, and just being a wonderful hostess. Fay also made arrangements for Pam and I to sleep in one of the rooms she had so carefully fixed up. I wouldn't offend the lady for anything but I had to say something. Pam and I had slept outside for most of the journey and could not possibly stay in a small room with not enough room to turn over in bed. I was most appreciative of her thoughtfulness, but I could not sleep under those conditions. Pam interceded and agreed. Fay did understand but she had no answer as to where we would sleep. I knew; that was the easy part. At first Fay said no, then we told her now we had been on the ground for so long that the carpet looked inviting. We slept there, got a good night's sleep and were ready to roll early.

In the northern part of Texas we continued to travel with beautiful scenery around us. The memory of west Texas and dry lands would stay and remind us to appreciate nature's garden more than ever.

The wagon train had grown to a large number of participants. We were all busy keeping horses and mules going. The heat was building, but not bad enough to stop us. We welcomed the new members but had so little time to get to know them. However, rewards came through the fact that we were all doing the same thing.

Since leaving Sulphur Springs, we were to have a diet of the same foods all along the trail. I am not saying it wasn't good, but it was usually the same. Vegetables were at a shortage everywhere on our plates. My sister-in-law met me in Nocona with pans and pans of her homegrown vegetables. She had brought a table with a table cloth, and she set up a spread that made me the envy of camp. We ate outside. Dee and Ruth Miller were there to join us. I can remember eating all the veggies I wanted for the first time in six months.

Helen Jones and Tooter Smith pulled out of our wagon train in Nocona. I would miss them very much. They had to return home and could not finish the ride. With them went a very bright shining light.

My daughter and grandson had adapted to the traveling schedule of the wagon train easily. They usually rode in Miss Hazel's wagon and had proven to be the kind of travelers that walked these grounds a century ago.

Muenster, Texas asked me to share my work of poems I had written along the trail and it was with appreciation I did so. The German community had been so very good to us.

Chapter Eighty-four

Our last three-day layover of the trip was in Gainsville. Wagons were being washed, horses groomed, harnesses cleaned. We were almost home. It did not seem like we had made as many miles as we knew we had. All the so-called experts had been wrong; the Texas Wagon Train had done the so-called impossible. We had made the trip. Suffered and persevered, we were the victors. It was hard not to gloat about it. As so many had made bets against us, so did they then become parted from their money.

All we really knew is that this great state had been built on a foundation as we had traveled; built on people with determination as we had, commitments, and pride and goals set to help Texas conquer any obstacle in her way. We knew how they did it; we knew how they over-came. To be out on the trail as we were is the only way to really absorb what the pioneers of the eighties did. Our comradary and fellowship will always hold us together even while we are all apart.

The Shivers family had traveled the miles of this journey not always under the best conditions. Always in the public's eye, they lived out of their wagons and sat up in the circle each night to be on display. Whether they wanted to or not was a necessity beyond their control. Fred and David did most of the hard labor while the wives watched over their families, four little girls with the oldest only five.

Denton, Texas is the home of their sponsor, Morrison Milling. We were coming into that town and preparations were being made to let the people of Denton know how well they had been represented through the Shivers families. The Mill was celebrating their on hundredth birthday also. Special planning had been put out to honor both the wagon representing the Morrison Mills and the family Mills. All of the Shivers hailed from Oklahoma but had represented this Texas based firm with Texas pride. In honor of these two families, I wrote a special poem for them and shared it with everyone at the ceremonies for them in Denton:

From the lands of Oklahoma,
All around the Lone Star State,
They left their homes and business
And did not hesitate.

Took a giant step in history,
Reached out to touch us all;

They've come three thousand miles
And did so standing tall.

Two big blue wagons rolling,
Five bays to pull their load,
Misfortune sometimes caught them
But they stayed out on the road.

From early in the mornings
We've seen them start their day,
Turn and help another;
Kindness is their pay.

Two brothers and their families
Will stop in Cowtown on the river.
They left a good impression.
We're all proud to know the Shivers.

Late the last night of our two-night stay in Denton, I was parked beside the trees of the campground and heard noises coming from the trees. It sounded like kids playing and I gave it not another thought. I had just turned off the lights and looked out to check on Lady, when all of a sudden I heard a horrible noise that sounded like the camper was going to be torn apart. I ran outside to see my mare caught under the pickup. I had no idea how she got there and from the thrashing she was doing, I knew at least two of her legs would be broken. I screamed as loud as I could to get help, and as God is witness, I do not know where all the helping hands came from. About twelve came running from out of nowhere in the dark. I did not have to say a word; they could tell by the sound what was wrong. One of the men called for a flashlight and jumped right in with the thrashing mare without thought of his own safety. She was fighting as hard as she could to get up as she was lodged under the truck. The stranger reached down with a knife and cut the rope twice as it was wound around her in more than one place. She jumped up and cut her nose on one of the braces of the camper. She had been tied to the camper since I got the unit in El Paso without any incident whatsoever. How this happened, I really don't know. She had never fought the line. It was then the noise from the trees came to mind. I think she must have been spooked by something or some-one. I checked her over closely to see what damage had been done. I could not find any marks but the one on her nose. What a stroke of luck that had been. Everyone that came to help disappeared into the night. I did not even get a chance to thank the man that helped the most. To my knowledge, I never saw him again.

Chapter Eighty-five

Only a few miles out of camp from Denton, we turned down a dirt country road. The trees reached up overhead of us and touching, made a perfect setting for the three thousand mile mark. The little bridge was narrow but the center of it was the exact line for the milestone. There was water flowing beneath the bridge in a small stream. The most unfortunate thing was the narrow road. All of the wagons could not be up front to be a part of the crossing. Mr. Oliver was there as were Quentin and Laurie. Pam Blanscet, Margaret Renz, and I were the only women that had left Sulphur Springs who were still riding horses—the only ones not on staff. Dorothy Allison, Viola Cook, and Vickie Hazzard had also done the same thing as members of our staff. I had written the traditional poem for the

occasion. With heavy emotions, I knew how everyone felt
at that moment, so I read to them my words, but couldn't
get rid of the lump in my throat:

> We've walked three thousand miles
> All around this big grand state,
> Watched millions of happy faces
> And we know now just what it takes
>
> To buy a freedom with a lifetime,
> Teach a child to thank the Lord,
> Bring back times in memory
> And what all the battles were fought for.
>
> From this day forward in your lives
> Keep all your thoughts from turning sour.
> Just bring to mind a wagon train
> And its bright and shining hour.
>
> Yes, we've walked three thousand miles
> Upon a road of modern times.
> And you know, the distance from last century
> Is just a narrow line.

Afterwards, the wagons passed over that little bridge
one by one so their pictures could be taken and recorded.
The first number of wagons were to be remembered as the
core of the wagon train. They were the people and teams
that had made the whole trip around the state. Wagons of
Jan France, Hazel Bown, Leo Miller, Rudi Nelson, Glenn
Pearce, Morrison Mills, Doug Kafka, Peggy White, Travis
Reeves, Cody Marketing, Betty McGahea, Bobby London,
Mr. and Mrs. Lun, Macey Nelson, Frances and Debbie
Johnson, Albert Nicely, Glenn Weeks, McCrosson Boys'
Ranch, James Simmons, Bill Tooley, Mr. and Mrs. Bagwell,

Al Winder, J. W. and Dort Jines, and so many many more that were just as important even if they did not travel the entire distance because of other commitments.

Pam, Margaret, and I rode out beside the lead wagon. Garry and Vern led the train and we walked another historic step over that little country bridge.

Chapter Eighty-six

June twenty-fifth, Ponder, Texas. A day all of the students had waited for. Their commencement exercises were to take place in that tiny town. We would have one student graduate off of the wagon train school. The school marm, Miss Anita, had prepared the occasion well. She had designed their report cards to be like no others would ever be again, a keepsake all of the students would treasure forever. Laurie Warner, the senior, was awarded her diploma and a scholarship to Texas Women's College. Parents and students were there in force, many of them in their best vintage clothes. I took a program after the exercises and walked amongst them to get all of the autographs. I could not see any difference between them and any top performer in the world. They were flattered, and I was honored.

The wagon train backtracked for a couple of miles to get into camp at Argyle. Our last talent show of the journey was held that night, coupled with planned talent that was to entertain us for the evening. We had a wonderful show. Argyle had done for the wagoneers what no one else had accomplished. They had made arrangements for the public not to overrun the camp. We loved the people that were always by our side to greet us. But the journey was quickly coming to an end. We wanted to selfishly enjoy our own and enjoy one of the final days together.

Our show started and the audience was the biggest. A young group of just teenagers played for us. They played old country music with a splash of the new. They were a refreshing group and we truly absorbed their entertainment. They played a few tunes, then one of our talented wagoneers would go forward to share with us their part in the program. We even got Quentin McGown to sing— that was a first! Woody, who had played her harmonica all around Texas, went forward and did a train song, one of our favorites, for the last time to our group. As she played, a train whistle was heard clearly in the background through the trees; the timing could not have been better. Mark our Purina man sang a new song he had written about the friendships we all had made out on the trail, a fine piece of work. I read a poem I had made for that night:

> We've almost come full circle,
> This covered wagon train,
> Walking into history,
> Feeling losses, feeling pain.
>
> Out across those hot dry flatlands,
> Up and down the hills so steep,
> Through thunder, rain, and lightning,
> Weary legs and weary feet.
>
> So many seem to ask us:
> "Are you tired of traveling on?"
> It's easy to say, "No,"
> And welcome them to come along.
>
> Friends from the past rejoin us,
> With open arms we take them in,
> Wish them well along their pathway
> And hope they stay until the end.

This has been a test of willpower
Between a human and a beast.
At times we want to quit
But refuse to face defeat.

Songbirds have entertained us,
Wildflowers greet us with a bend,
Freedom's been our partner,
And there is music in the wind.

Wagoneers would linger in one another's camps a little longer. It was natural. I myself wanted to get around to get addresses. Until the very end, I did not get this done. My relatives made me a very special hand-stitched cloth just to use as autograph/address sheet. I will take it to the first reunion. Pam Blanscet was still insisting she was going to ride Duke into Billy Bob's when the train pulled into the stockyards. It sounded like a good idea to me. After all, people had been riding horses into bars since the days of the old West.

After Gainsville, Whitsboro was added to our schedule. The town was most excited to have our group into their area. They erected a monument and walked down the streets crying because of feelings about this group. We were already emotional about coming to an end. I believe Whitesboro could feel that too. The final days of our trip saw the numbers grow so big we did not know who was who. The newcomers must have thought we were a prudish bunch. We weren't but the last minute details to bring the wagons into the stockyards was time-consuming. Plus, from Argyle to Fort Worth, a sea of people were our constant companions.

Chapter Eighty-seven

We had traveled days, weeks, and months. The enthusiasm we were met with as we passed along the trail each day will never be forgotten. On the day that we would go thirty and forty miles, we were tired and wanted just to have a bite to eat then turn in for the night. But the people along the roadway were always there to smile, wave, and reach out to us. Our thoughts of calling it a day would be wiped away with the wave of a tiny hand or the tears of joy flowing down the face of someone that had lived many years, a life that could never be duplicated, but the wagon train brought their lives before them, one more time. We knew those people were in the final autumn of their years. How could we not return the same enthusiasm as they had given us. This electricity followed us everywhere and never at any time of the journey did anyone on the train fail to receive these greetings in the manner of which they were sent out to us gratefully.

Chapter Eighty-eight

On our way to Lewisville, we had a lunch stop with all the trimmings, cold drinks, hamburgers. We are under trees and were served by volunteers who showed appreciation toward us. Again one could argue who was the most grateful to see who. I was asked to share three of my poems with our welcomers by the committee women. My cousins Ann, Lorraine, and Aunt Florence came and took me on into camp from there. We camped right on Lewisville Lake. My campsite was just a stone's throw from the water's edge. Ann then drove me back out to the city blocks were the train would pass. I stood on the corner and told my friends I was going to have a nice hot shower with all the hot water I wanted and I should see them later. A lot of "boos" came back at me. I laughed . . . all the way to the shower.

Our countdown had begun. We were less than a week from the end of the trail.

Chapter Eighty-nine

Lady had started to show a swelled left ankle. I knew it was a result of the mishap in Denton. She had come all that way without a single leg problem—only to be injured in camp. I would ride in one wagon or another until the morning we were to ride into the stockyards. I would ride her if I had to pump her full of pain killer.

Irving is the home of the Texas Wagon train headquarters. The wagon train was very well taken care of there at the Cowboy Center, one of Trilands projects. Plus Rudi Nelson, driver of the Triland Stagecoach, was to be married in the circle of wagons. After the wagoneers were settled into camp for the night's stay, we all gathered in the circle. Jana was driven in, in the stagecoach. She was helped out and walked the red carpet to her waiting groom. When the minister ask if anyone objected, I could not resist calling out, "Go for it, Rudi!" They both returned to the stage and disappeared to an unknown destination. No telling what may have happened to that happy couple if we wagoneers could have found them.

T-Bone steaks were served to us, and Charlie Pride was there for our entertainment. He put on a fabulous show to a huge crowd of pioneers. Thanks, Charlie Pride, you were wonderful!

Moving into the campgrounds in The Grapevine/Colleyville area allowed us to gather together and exchange addresses, for those who remembered to do so. I went over to have watermelon with Miss Hazel and Viola Cook. It really was time for the journey to end. The weather had turned hot. We were all worn to a frazzle, even those that would not admit to it. Viola and I sat and visited a while. She was the head outrider just as she had been on the Bicentennial wagon train to Valley Forge, Pennsylvania in 1976. She rode a Paso Fino horse this trip. It had been born on the Bicentennial train. Viola had been a horse trainer and trick rider for many years. She has donated her time on many occasions to the underprivileged, and given her spirit to aid others in the horse world almost her entire life. Viola Cook was nominated into the Cowboy Hall of Fame since the end of the wagon train. A great honor. Viola and her faithful mount Freedom were always on the trail trying to keep order in a group that would just as soon not pay her the time of day. It is not easy to please all. Viola just tried. She gave her legs to the sport of rodeo. Freedom has no sight. Together they made the steps of this journey with the help only from each other.

Chapter Ninety

North Richland Hills put us at the Greenway Racetrack. We had a two-day layover. Coming into the campgrounds brought the wagon train in the back entrance. This in turn put us coming down the racetrack. I was riding in the Shivers wagon, we decided to have some fun again. Fred rode out to greet us from camp on horseback. We suggested to him to go back and tell Doug Kafka, driving the Wrangler wagon, that we should race. Doug took the suggestion and pulled right up beside Morrison Milling. By appearances sake we looked as if we were both racing down the track toward camp—just another mischievous act that couldn't be passed up.

Carl Vaughan entertained us that night in camp at the dance—more talk about the end of the trail. It was always on our minds now. A sadness had seeped into our atmosphere.

The final branding of the wagons with the wagon train brand took place the second day. I had not had anything branded with the wagon brand, therefore, I carried my saddle and chaps out to the branding fire. As usual, Kenny Taylor was working hard to get the job done. He had already branded all the wagons that were entitled to it. What a proud bunch it was that stood by their rigs to receive that third wagon train brand. They had traveled the required three thousand miles and the symbol of their efforts was burned permanently into the sides of their historic vehicles. In my case, I had the three brands burned into my saddle and my chaps. My chaps were the only pair that had the YO, the Pitchfork, and the 6666 burned into them plus the three wagons. Bobby had taken them to the headquarters while we were camped on the Four Six ranch and had them branded. I did not know this. He surprised me with it later. The Four Six did not bring out their branding equipment as the others had done. My husband took his request to one of the hands that he knew and they obliged. The brander said they had not done a pair of chaps before. I am most proud of this possession. The branding at Greenway, took most of the day. Mother nature did her part: the rains came.

Fred and Mildred Stroade, of Balmorea, came into camp. I had received a letter from Fred stating they would be in Fort Worth at the end of the trail. This came only after Fred had assured me there was no way he would be in the stockyards because of the heavy traffic and to many people. I had to rib him about this, as the first line of the letter read: "They would be at the Holiday Inn." They are special friends and I was thrilled to have them there. They came looking for me in the driving rain. Now this would take a good friend to face that. We met under the canopy of the Morrison Milling wagon.

Chapter Ninety-one

I was keeping a close watch on Lady. I wanted to ride her but the swelling was still in her ankle. Mrs. Parker, my landlady, sent an ointment out with Bobby and we wrapped the leg in hopes she would heal. We dined on fish and chips or barbecued food at Greenway. I worried about the baby and the heat, but he was doing great. Donya was a little uncomfortable. We knew what the original pioneers must have felt. They did not have any way to cool off or escape the insects. We were being plagued with mosquitos. Some of the wagoneers had air conditioned units; I was not one of them. But I always found a big tree to park under.

I rode in the lead wagon. My daughter and my grandson rode in the second wagon as we came into the city of Fort Worth. The wagons would stay at Gateway Park one night before moving into the famous stockyards. It was important to me to be aware of this crossing. I was the only woman that had traveled the distance, riding a horse, from Fort Worth. I felt like I was coming home and bringing my friends, a bunch of them, with me. Bobby had accepted the invitation from O. C. Horn to ride in his wagon, but he was moving up the vehicles the last week for other wagoneers besides ours and just wasn't able to fulfill his word. He would see it that Jimmy Daniel's truck was moved up because Jimmy and Mike Jackson had moved my mare up for me from camp to camp while she was recuperating from her injury. Jimmy had let me ride in his wagon whenever I wanted to and I appreciated everything he had graciously done.

As we passed by the crowds of people along the streets coming into Fort Worth, I could not hold back the tears. From the two little girls dressed like the Statue of Liberty to the two elderly ladies sitting in front of the retirement home they both lived in, holding an old American flag across their laps and waving small Texas flags. I caught my breath continuously. People were at every step of the way. I thought of many things that day of travel. I knew I was not alone with my thoughts. So many miles we had traveled against a lot of odds along with alot of negative thinkers. All of that did not matter now; we were in Fort Worth. I wiped more tears when I saw the skyline of the downtown area. Yes, we had really come full circle. It was great to see familiar landmarks and turn a corner and know, for once, where I was. We had passed through town after town in the past six months, I had always asked for directions to get from one point to another. Now I did not have to do that. A goal had been set, a commitment met. Damn! I was proud of these people! I jumped off of the wagon at our lunch stop just inside the city limits and ran around hugging everybody, welcoming them to *my* town and wiping tears. I'd come home.

We rolled on toward our camp at Gateway Park, down a back picturesque roadway that is one of the most beautiful in Fort Worth. The trees touched above our heads like protective hands from the master. I wiped more tears as I knew we were all being enfolded. I kept looking back down the street to see my friends come up around the turns.

Fort Worth had met us and was out in force to see this event into their town. We made the left hand turn into the campgrounds down the dirt road to where the trees stood, off to our left into Gateway Park. I gasped at what I saw. There beneath the trees, standing beside a little green wagon, was a light sorrel draft horse. It was Pam Burchell's outfit. I had said it all along, Pam would come into the stockyards with us. Her hat was still hanging in the lead wagon. She had come with me and my friends. My tears flowed along with the rest of the wagoneers; none of us could help it. Pam's husband, Stan, would drive the wagon the next day into the stockyards along with his two children to fulfill the dream of his wife, that had cost them all dearly. That night, we had ceremonies to welcome us to Fort Worth. Recognition went out to the sponsors for helping us meet the payroll. The governor walked amongst us and also spoke to us of our accomplishment. We had been allowed a five day grace period along the trail to miss and still be counted as a full time wagoneer. I am not saying that the job of the companions traveling with or helping the wagoneers get the wagons rolling each morning was not important, because it was, or many of them could not have made this trip. But we had made this goal in the beginning and there were those of us that reached inside of ourselves to accomplish this commitment no matter what. Twenty-one wagoneers met the challenge and were recognized for doing such. I was one of them and proud of it. Only two women on horseback had made the mark: Margaret Renz and me. We were called to the front to receive our plaques. "Yes", I cried.

It was all coming to an end. Jan and Garry gave me a wonderful award for being the most inspirational cheerleader of the journey.

Coburn's Cafeteria of Fort Worth provided and served

the wagoneers with a wonderful dinner, complete with commemorative scarves synonymous to our arrival. The band played on into the night; music was heard throughout the trees and camps for the last time. The wagon train would go on into Saginaw after leaving Fort Worth. But two separate groups were going on to Sulphur Springs to actually complete the circle around the state. People like Elmo and Helen Lun who had driven down from Gailsville, Wisconsin in their wagon with the same team of horses that had pulled them around the state, were to return home the same way. The team would take them back to Gailsville. They would be on the road more than fifteen months and have logged more than six thousand miles. The Luns would want to get started back home as soon as possible. They had been wonderful people to travel with and had represented their state very well.

The Gateway camp was huge. I was under the trees alongside the Trinity River. Lady was ready to go. The medicine Mrs. Parker had sent out to me did the trick. I walked out amongst the campgrounds and the circle of wagons that night. I knew it would never be this size or the same again. I listened to the sounds of the night, as well as the music drifting out across the canvas tops. I could hear the livestock communicating with one another one last time before bedding down. Many new wagons had pulled into camp. I did not know any of the new people and knew I never would. They had come in by such numbers it was incredible. One hundred fifty-nine wagons would roll out of camp the next morning, to stretch more than two miles down the streets of Fort Worth to be met by thousands and thousands of welcomers. Time was slipping by. I wanted it to stop, to hold this moment in time a little longer. This journey had meant a lot to me as I knew it had to others. As I stood in the circle, I pivoted around wanting to cling to that last night, that last sight of what had been a way of life to me and my friends for so many miles, and such excitement we would never re-create again together. I returned to my camp late in the evening. Most of the lights were already out. It was to be an emotional day to follow. Boyd Ivey was still going strong with his tools of his trade: ringing the anvil and hammering the horseshoes.

Chapter Ninety-two

July 3. Our last few miles into the stockyards was not many. Garry was not to give "wagons ho" until ten that morning. It was hard to come to terms with as we had rolled out for so long at seven. The stock was to stand around in their harnesses and saddles long before depar-ture. Old habits were hard to break. I was handed a Fort Worth City flag and asked to ride next to the lead wagon on the left side. I also put on my chaps depicting my symbols of accomplishments. I pulled my hat down for the rain had started to fall. I was going to get very wet but refused to put on a rainslick. The temperature was warm and my rainslick was already in the next camp. Lady was feeling good; her ankle showed no signs of injury. I stepped into the saddle and rode the circle one more time, carrying the Fort Worth flag, greeting everyone by name as I had done for so many miles. When I got to the wagons that I was unfamiliar with, I just said good morning anyway; they all reciprocated and our journey began.

The rain poured on our parade, yet there was no way even that amount of moisture could wash away the smiles. Mixed with the tears, we left Gateway Park and entered into the moments of finality.

My father-in-law and mother-in-law were celebrating their fifty-seventh wedding anniversary on that day. They were to be waiting on the corner of First Street and Riverside. Bobby was there as well with the rest of my family. I told Jan about the anniversary. She said to be sure and let her knew a bit ahead of time and she would have the entire wagon load of people with her call out their greetings to my in-laws.

The rain poured and poured. Our spirits were high and one would have thought the sun was shining brightly. We were approaching the Cavenaugh house. I called to Jan. She turned and had everyone call out: "Happy Anniversary Frances and Loney Stepp!" They stood and waved. Donya and the baby were in the second wagon with Miss Hazel. My tears were well hidden with the rain. Bobby stood on the curb holding up a big sign welcoming me home with my friends. What a wonderful feeling.

On toward downtown we rolled. The streets were lined with welcomers calling to us and congratulating the wagoneers for a job well done. Walt Garrison, our honorary wagon master, rode in front with Charles Oliver directly behind Garry and Vern.

The rain kept coming and so did we. Circling the courthouse downtown, we rolled out over the bridge behind it, out main street toward Billy Bob's. The people were there mile after mile. We waved and returned their good cheer. I saw familiar faces and friends. The thought kept repeating itself in my mind: We did it! We did it!

Coming down Main Street toward the stockyards, we passed the North Fort Worth Bank. My friend Shirley worked there and I wanted to call out to her, but the crowd was so thick I couldn't find her. We made the turn onto Exchange Avenue. The people were thirty deep on the streetsides, calling and reaching out to us. Lady became nervous when I pulled the flag out of the boot to wave at the crowd. I didn't get it back for a moment and she went crazy with all of the noise. We had paraded through many a town together, but the crowd never reached and touched us before in such numbers. I slipped the flag in the boot, reached down, and touched her. She settled down and walked easy alongside the crowds just inches away.

Fort Worth was meeting us as no others had, I will never forget the crowd. I rode Lady as close to the wagon as I could get. We turned and came up Rodeo Drive. The entire stockyard area had been renovated while we were making our way around the state. It was beautiful and made complete with the Texas wagon train winding its way to camp. Tall and proud we were. We had made it!

I rode off to the side while the wagons turned into the circle area. I wanted to see my friends come around the corner. Wagon after wagon passed by; I called out to each one. Their expressions of accomplishment and pride, coupled with smiles of success, and of course the tears were overwhelming. O. C. Horn passed by and as I waved and yelled at he and Kathryn, I saw Bobby in the wagon right beside Kathryn. Donya and Preston were already in place in the circle. My son Damon could not make it in to ride with me the last few days, but he was on my mind.

Chapter Ninety-three

Since we had left Abilene, Fred Shivers and Mr. Oliver started to put together the auction to be held in the arena in Cowtown Coliseum the next day. The auction was to help the wagoneers that wanted to recoup some of the money they had spent to make the journey. It was not easy putting together an event such as the auction from the road, but with a little help from his friends, he did it. Fred and Debbie have held auctions before and were familiar with the format. I was recruited because of my experience working at the Fort Worth Auto Auction prior to leaving on the wagon train. Professional auctioneers were brought in to help; Fred, Debbie and I were to assist wherever we were needed. Fred worked into the night to get the arena set up and ready to go.

Debbie and I handled a lot of paper work; Fred worked the floor. Just before the auction began, Eugene Bond, the one who handled our public relations area, arranged to take me up to the band on the stage overlooking the arena to ask them to play a traditional piece while I read the last poem I had written for the end of the trail. I originally wanted to save this one until we reached the final campground in Saginaw, but so many were to leave the next morning, I chose to share it the first time with everyone there. I had read the poem several times and once even to Helen Jones as she left our camp for the last time in Nocona.

But I still did not know if I could read it successfully before those many wagoneers, the public, and all without getting choked. But I tried:

    Now the anvils are silent,
    The wagon wheels have stopped.
    Our journey has ended;
    The last mile's been walked.

    Empty are saddles
    With horses close by,
    History's been made
    Beneath the blue Texas sky.

From deep in our hearts
We've grown close with such pride;
Now we go home
With each tear that we've cried.

This journey was made
For the young and the old;
They lit up the roadway
The further we rolled.

Thunder and lightning,
Windstorms and Heat;
The wagoneers conquered;
There was no defeat.

Bluebonnets, Piney Woods,
Red dusty roads,
Bridges we've crossed,
Stories to be told.

Men and women alike,
We came from the past;
Gathering memories;
We're safe here at last.

Hard work and sweat,
Tension and pain;
We all worked together
And we'd do it again.

We can't say good-bye,
For it's hard, don't you know?
Lets just say "happy trails"
Til the next "WAGONS HO!"

The crowd had loved it. I was crying. I knew Bobby wiped a tear or two. Jan wasn't any better. Dow Jones and The Stock Exchange band had done an excellent job. Throughout the day and the auction, friends and strangers stopped by the podium where I worked on the arena floor to thank me for doing the poem for them. All I could say was, it was my pleasure to create the words for everyone.

For the two nights in the stockyards, the wagoneers celebrated. They all did their own thing and suffered their own way through the next morning. It was a good celebration however. Pam had kept her promise; she rode Duke into Billy Bob's out onto the dance floor. She was arrested for it and escorted to the local holding facility where, I must add, Quentin went to bat for her and had her released. I thought it was wrong for her to be arrested in the first place. How else does one end a historic journey if not by riding one's horse into a bar in the Fort Worth Stockyards?

For those of us who continued on to Saginaw, we rolled out the morning of the fifth. We were twenty-four wagons and fifty-nine horseback riders. Saginaw rolled out the red carpet for the end of the trail. We were quartered on the Windy Ryon Memorial rodeo grounds and enjoyed our final night together. A feed for the wagoneers was furnished in town. James Watson had written a song entitled "Wagons Ho." I read a piece I had written about Pam Burchell and the proceeds of the record sales went to her family.

I awoke early Sunday morning, the sixth, to bid Garry and Jan a safe journey as they took their small band of wagons on to Sulphur Springs to complete the circle and go home. I was going to ride my mare the last seven miles to my house.

I saddled up at eight A.M. and rode out. Bobby followed me in the car along the freeway, my protector from the modern-day world. We had to cross the Lake Worth Bridge northwest of Fort Worth. Waiting until the traffic was clear, I urged the mare onto the narrow traffic way that was under construction. She started to hesitate at the narrowness of it, plus the heavy vehicle traffic passing close by, but a little gentle verbal coaxing sent us on our way. I took a deep breath to help swallow a large lump in my throat. I was most proud of Lady. She had done a good job against a lot of odds and other people's opinions.

Just a mile from the house, she and I heard a mule bray off in the trees. She whirled around with lightning quick movements. She was looking for the wagon train. I reached and patted her. With tears in my eyes, I spoke to her because I wanted her to know I was going to miss them too.

I gave her the signal five hundred yards from the house. We raced on toward home. A lonely rider along an interstate highway, deep in the heart of America.

Epilogue

If everyone who reads this story felt, just once, the dedication and sacrifice our forefathers laid down for this country and for Texas, then our journey was a total success. For those foundations of strength are obviously still in our heritage and will continue to shine through for generations to come. I have done without and not suffered. The pioneers of the eighties walked in the footsteps and shadows of the original settlers from so many years ago. No one even knows who all of them were.

Just let it go down in history that those people entered into a way of life, a standard of living, that may have changed throughout the moments of time, then passed through their lives and on into the lives of the pioneers of the eighties.

Through these mighty early citizens, corporations have given birth to expand across America. Tiny towns have met the challenges of modern-day expansions, and time has not stood still. The Texas Wagon Train walked over three thousand miles, bringing to life the past that has made this country the strongest country in the world.

I know now where it all began; I was there. Through the combined efforts of all the people in this book, and many more, we brought the light from the past and shared it not only with our proud fellow Texans, but with all of the men and women of America who can look into the past and see just where that very light we carried so far, came from, and thank God every day for the freedoms that were paid for, one hundred fifty years ago with men, women, and children's lives.

As brotherhood is, you cannot touch it, but it's always there. Did they know, then, where these steps were taking them? They had to. For without a positive attitude toward their future, the wagons would never have rolled. Reaching back into the years as we have these past months, we touched those early settlers, and they touched us. For those who believe the frontiers are now only in space, you can't convince us who rode the wagon train. There isn't any frontier left here on Mother Earth.

On the Trail

Bruce Clemmens, of Bracketville, Texas, lifetime member of
the U.S. Cavalry.

The official horsehshoer, Boyd Ivey, of Dekalb, Texas. He built the wagon behind him and was usually seen without his "bonnet."

Every team of horses and mules needed to be held by a wagoneer as we crossed the Livingston Reservoir. Here Frances Lembauch leads the Whitfield wagon.

Macy Nelson, of Alpha, Illinois. Everyone called him Santa Claus.

Branding on the YO Ranch.

All of the materials to make this wreath were found on the road by Cotton Williams, of Donaldson, Arkansas.

Debbie and Teresa Shivers traveled with their families and lived out of their wagons. Always in the public eye, they were true pioneer wives from Oklahoma.

Another pioneer woman was Debbie Johnson, of Henrietta, Texas accompanied by her son Nathan.

These signs were with us on our journey—not the usual road signs, unless traveling by our method.

Pam Burchell's wagon and draft mare, Barbie. We lost Pam on January 25, 1986. She was from Newark, Texas.

John Gilbert drove one of our "Blue Rooms" the entire journey. His air-conditioned, heated, radio-equipped John Deere made it a little easier.

Garry France, the wagon master, leading the train with the official pacesetter. Garry is in the foreground.

Charlie Welch, of Midland, Texas, with the largest team on the trail—Peter and Piper, both English Shires.

Kay Lightfoot, of Hurricane Mills, Tennessee. She and I put the flag corps together.

Lyle Heber, of South Dakota. He and I made quite the pair at our Easter Egg Hunt in Balmorea, Texas.

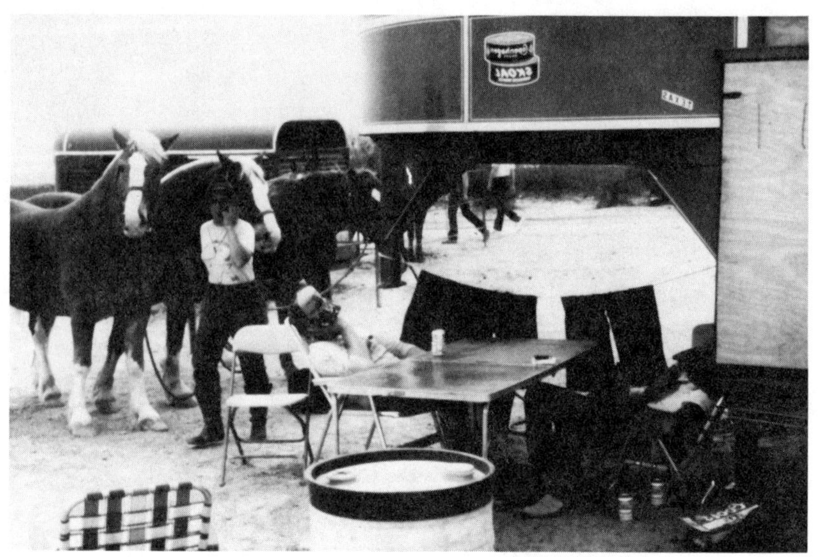

Women's work was never done. The men were all worn out from a rough game of poker.

Vern Renz rode every step of the way. Indian Creek, Texas, is very proud of their mailman.

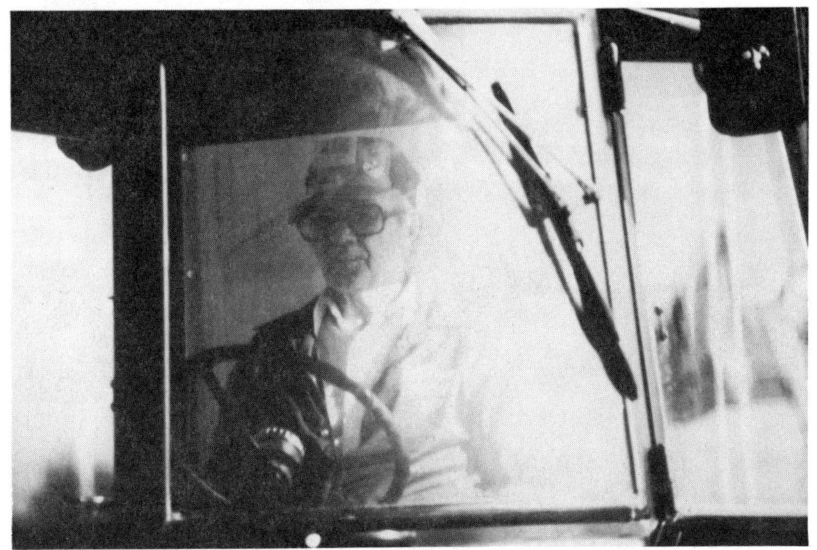

Cecil Dobkins kept the second John Deere going, bringing up the rear.

Tending the wheels to keep the wagons rolling was a daily scene.

Pat Weeks, of Simms, Texas, fills one of the three water tanks from the mother tank.

This kind of dust blew us along for five hundred miles.

Hazel Bowen, of Antelope, Texas, has held a set of lines in her hands for over seventy-five years.

James Whitfield chose not to mount a horse, but kept the listeners going with his ham radio transmitting.

Riders and wagons ready to roll out onto the roadway from a water stop.

Al Walker, of Sulphur, Oklahoma, and an assistant rechecking the gear for the day's ride.

The Texas Wagon Train crossing the Pitchfork Ranch. It was often easy to turn thoughts back to a century ago.

Myself and my mare Lucky Lady enjoying a lunch stop.

Ina Nell "Woody" Wood, of North Richland Hills, Texas, entertained many wagoneers with her harmonica.

The author reading the final poem in the Coliseum in the Fort Worth stockyards.

Fred Shivers helped his daughters auction off their "stick Horses" at our trail's end auction. His niece Abbra Shivers is also in the picture. The rest of us must have done something wrong. The stick horses brought thousands of dollars.

SCHEDULE OF ROUTE

Town or Camp	Date	Day of Week	Mileage
Sulphur Springs (Civic Center)	1-2	Thurs	
Como/Pickton	1-2	Thurs	15
Winnsboro	1-3	Fri	11
Quitman	1-4	Sat	16
Hawkins	1-5	Sun	21
Gladewater	1-6	Mon	14
Longview	1-7-8	Tues,Wed	15
Marshall	1-9-10	Thurs,Fri	31
Carthage	1-11	Sat	18
Clayton	1-12	Sun	18
Mount Enterprise	1-13	Mon	22
Macogdoches	1-14-15	Tues,Wed	23
Lufkin	1-16-17	Thurs,Fri	20
Corrigan	1-18	Sat	22
Livingston	1-19	Sun	22
Camilia	1-20	Mon	12
San Jacinto Nat. Forest	1-21	Tues	24
Conroe	1-22-23	Wed,Thurs	14
Montgomery	1-24	Fri	24
Tomball	1-25	Sat	34
Hockley	1-26	Sun	15
Hempstead	1-27-28	Mon,Tues	18.5
Brenham	1-29	Wed	25
Carmine	1-30	Thurs	20
Giddings	1-31	Fri	19
Elgin	2-1	Sat	34
Austin N/E 290	2-2	Sun	15
Austin South 183	2-3-4	Mon,Tues	22
Mendoza (Archie Roberts Ranch)	2-5	Wed	23
Luling	2-6	Thurs	12
Gonzales	2-7	Fri	19
Cheapside	2-8	Sat	20
Cuero	2-9-10	Sun,Mon	18
Open Camp	2-11	Tues	14
Goliad	2-12	Wed	15
Refugio	2-13	Thurs	25
Sinton	2-14	Fri	26
Robstown	2-15	Sat	23
Kingsville	2-16-17-18	Sun,Mon,Tues	30
Alice	2-19	Wed	31
San Diego	2-20-21	Thurs,Fri	14
Freer	2-22	Sat	25
Open Camp	2-23	Sun	19
Tilden	2-24	Mon	23
Christine (Duncan Hirsh Ranch)	2-25	Tues	25
Poteet	2-26	Wed	20
San Antonio	2-27	Thurs	20.9
San Antonio (Freeman Coliseum)	2-28, 3-1	Fri,Sat	21
San Antonio	3-2	Sun	22
Spring Branch	3-3	Mon	25
Johnson City	3-4	Tues	22
L B J State Park	3-5	Wed	15

SCHEDULE OF ROUTE

Town or Camp	Date	Day of Week	Mileage
Fredericksburg	3-6	Thurs	19
Kerrville	3-7	Fri	27
Hunt	3-8	Sat	18
Felix Kline Ranch	3-9	Sun	16
YO Ranch	3-10-11	Mon,Tues	21
Junction	3-12	Wed	20
Seiker Ranch	3-13	Thurs	19
Menard	3-14	Fri	22
Eden	3-15	Sat	22
Eola	3-16	Sun	25
San Angelo	3-17-18	Mon,Tues	25
San Angelo (Twin Buttes)	3-19	Wed	15
Mertzon	3-20	Thurs	18
Bernhart	3-21	Fri	28
Big Lake	3-22-23	Sat,Sun	19
Rankin	3-24	Mon	30
McCamey	3-25	Tues	19
Open Camp	3-26	Wed	25
Fort Stockton	3-27-28	Thurs,Fri	27
Open Camp	3-29	Sat	27
Balmorhea	3-30	Sun	28.1
Open Camp	3-31	Mon	17
Kent	4-1	Tues	17
Open Camp	4-2	Wed	13
Van Horn	4-3-4	Thurs,Fri	24
Allamore	4-5	Sat	12
Sierra Blanca	4-6	Sun	24
Fort Quitman	4-7	Mon	20
Fort Hancock	4-8-9	Tues,Wed	16
Tornillo	4-10	Thurs	18
San Elizario	4-11	Fri	13
El Paso	4-12-13-14	Sat,Sun,Mon	18
Open Camp	4-15	Tues	24
Smith Ranch	4-16	Wed	10
Cornudas	4-17	Thurs	27
Salt Flat	4-18	Fri	24
Open Camp	4-19	Sat	19
Guadalupe Nat. Park	4-20-21-22	Sun,Mon,Tues	6
Old Polly Holobeke Ranch	4-23	Wed	21
Bob Farmer Ranch	4-24	Thurs	19
Orla	4-25	Fri	20
Mentone	4-26	Sat	27
Kermit	4-27-28	Sun,Mon	34
Notrees	4-29	Tues	23
Odessa	4-30,5-1	Wed,Thurs	25
Midland	5-2	Fri	23
Open Camp	5-3	Sat	19
Patricia	5-4	Sun	26
Lamesa	5-5-6	Mon,Tues	21
O'Donnell	5-7	Wed	19
Tahoka	5-8	Thurs	15
Lubbock /	5-9	Fri	38

SCHEDULE OF ROUTE

Town or Camp	Date	Day of Week	Mileage
Levelland	5-10	Sat	28
Littlefield	5-11	Sun	25
Spring Lake	5-12-13	Mon, Tues	23
Dimmitt	5-14	Wed	22
Hereford	5-15	Thurs	24
Canyon	5-16	Fri	34
Amarillo	5-17-18-19	Sat, Sun, Mon	26
Claude	5-20	Tues	23
Ashtola	5-21	Wed	23
Clarendon	5-22	Thurs	10
Brice	5-23	Fri	18.4
Turkey	5-24-25	Sat, Sun	24.5
Matador	5-26	Mon	21
Glenn	5-27	Tues	16.4
Dickens	5-28	Wed	27
Pitchfork Ranch	5-29-30	Thurs, Fri	22
6666 Ranch	5-31	Sat	15
Benjamin	6-1-2	Sun, Mon	26.4
Rochester	6-3	Tues	18
Haskell	6-4	Wed	22
Stamford	6-5	Thurs	15
Anson	6-6	Fri	25
Abilene	6-7-8	Sat, Sun	16.4
Albany	6-9	Mon	24.6
Fort Griffin	6-10	Tues	24
Throckmorton	6-11	Wed	20.4
Olney	6-12	Thurs	22.2
Archer City	6-13	Fri	19
Windthorst	6-14	Sat	11
Wichita Falls	6-15-16	Sun, Mon	27
Henrietta	6-17	Tues	20
Nacona	6-18	Wed	32
Muenster	6-19	Thurs	23
Gainesville	6-20-21	Fri, Sat	13
Whitesboro	6-22	Sun	15
Pilot Point	6-23	Mon	20
Denton	6-24	Tues	10
Ponder	6-25	Wed	12
Argyle	6-26	Thurs	16
Lewisville	6-27	Fri	21
Irving	6-28	Sat	15
Grapevine/Collyville	6-29	Sun	11
North Richland Hills	6-30, 7-1	Mon, Tues	14
Gateway Park (Forth Worth)	7-2	Wed	15
Fort Worth Stockyards	7-3-4	Thurs, Fri	5
Saginaw	7-5-6	Sat, Sun	5